Journeys
With Horses

By
Leslie McDonald

REVIEWS

"Clearly written by a true horseperson, with correct jargon and descriptions of breeds, disciplines, and venues, this book has stories about war heroes, little girls dreaming of ponies, The Temple Lipizzans, trail rides gone awry, and much more. I plan to give this to all my horsey friends! (and maybe some non-horsey ones too)" **Lydia Gray, Ilinois. Author of Classical Dressage Foundations with Wolfgang May.**

"In our lives, we have many paths from which to choose - and each journey is as special and unique as the individuals themselves. For the fortunate few, the shared partner on the journey is our equine companion where our most treasured moments include strength, passion, dreams and rewards. The review staff at Equineinfoexchange.com feels enriched by the many journeys so vividly described and brought to life by Leslie McDonald. We capture diversity at EIE, and appreciate the breadth of scale offered by Ms. McDonald in **Journeys With Horses** with the range of colorful and compelling stories to provide the reader with an array of adventures. Be brave and be a part of these cherished journeys. You will enjoy the remarkable ride." **The review staff at the largest global directory for everything equine http://equineinfoexchange.com.**

Photo Credit:

Photo credit for interior photos - Doug Froh
Cover artwork by Leslie McDonald

Leslie McDonald
c/o Down the Aisle Promotions
http://fcfarm.com

Leslie is also the author of the following books:

Down the Aisle
Musings of a Horse Farm Corgi
Making Magic
Tic-Tac
Personally autographed copies are available at
http://fcfarm.com

Retail Price: $12.95
Printed in the USA

TABLE OF CONTENTS

DEDICATION

Dedicated to those who have come before

and those still yet to come who inspire, support,

and believe in the journey.

INTRODUCTION

O ur journeys with horses follow many diverse paths. Some people are drawn young down the aisle for a childhood fix inspired by fantasies born in the stirrups of a red rocking horse. They often retreat early when the whim is sated, moving on to pursue professional careers or families where, by necessity, horses fade to a fond memory, occasionally taken out and dusted off with friends who chose a similar ground-bound path.

Other journeys are based upon dreams that seem impossible to achieve in a childhood world that doesn't include the space or finances for horses. Despite a driving desire, they are often thwarted from beginning their journey until middle years. But, when their ultimate dream is finally attained, the reward is oh-so-much sweeter than any adolescent's immature cravings could ever be.

Then there is the journey of those drawn to the aisle by an insatiable passion. They are the ones determined to carve out their personal groove no matter the physical cost or emotional sacrifice. Without the horses who occupy their every waking thought, their lives would never seem fulfilled.

A life lived fully down the aisle is defined by stories that are personal markers of the journey. Some are clear constants, lingering on the fringe as shadowy memories, while others fade away to be buried deep in the subconscious. There they dwell, forgotten by the passage of time, until unexpectedly reawakened by something as simple as an "oldie" blaring from the shelf radio, or the scent of freshly oiled leather, or a tri-colored foxhound baying in the distance just after sunrise, or even the fragrance of fence line honeysuckle brushed by a morning canter.

Decades of treasured memories stack atop faded, dust-tinged photos and ribbons lining tack room walls, the gathered accumulation of a horse lover's life. Until one day, without warning, the unexpected surprise of a forgotten marker is triggered into consciousness. The pleasure of unwrapping that long-ago marker is one to be slowly savored with the fresh perspective of age and time, run across remembrance like a breeze rustling the leaves of memory.

Some are life-altering events, such as wiping clear the nostrils of a newborn filly, her hind legs still resting inside a beloved mare before the final push; or a face pressed against the midnight glass of an operating room as the vet turns from a horse's colic belly incision to give a positive thumbs up; or watching the sturdy wooden trusses finally being erected for the long-dreamed-of indoor arena.

Other markers are smaller snapshot moments, but equally as powerful in memory. A thirteen-year-old's pit-of-the-stomach terror at the first gallop down to a looming telephone pole jump, followed instantly upon safe landing by the "I did it!" euphoric fist pump; or a lunge line confidence-building lesson overcoming the fears of a tentative student partnered with a trusted black mare; or training in the shade of ringside trees planted over the years in memory of special horses whose generosity and expertise laid the foundation for the newest bright prospect to sport the farm logo on his saddle pad.

Every marker tells the tale of the scent, the sight and the sensations of the stable aisle that is the horse lover's world. They are stories reawakened to be treasured, savored, and rekindled close to the heart. Perhaps within these pages you will discover a marker that triggers your memory and pause to remember that special experience or person who inspired your own journey down the aisle with horses.

CHAPTER ONE
AISLE 2

G rooms are a mixed lot, drawn down the aisle from all walks of life. Some scurry to the stable to feed equine passions, hoping hard labor will offset personal financial limitations with a leg up through the sawdust ceiling. Careers are built out of cramped back-aisle apartments, where early mornings are jump-started by the kick of a hot pot caffeine fix and a microwaved cherry pop tart. In pursuit of future glory, they willingly shovel, groom, and braid their way up the stable food chain in hopes of replacing muck forks and rubber curry combs with fine English leather between their legs.

For some it serves as a temporary adolescent summer break, recharging from nine months of structured schoolroom studies. It becomes a brief respite to fill the soul with the rich aromas of leather, tanbark, and horse sweat before stepping back into September's "real world" academic responsibilities.

Others remain invisible, not staying long enough in one place for their names to become imprinted on the boarders' memories. They shove faded t-shirts into well-worn jeans, unwilling or unable to make a long-term commitment as they drift from stable to track to breeding shed, chasing the promise of the perfect job on ads posted in feed mills or on the internet.

And then there are those for whom the profession becomes a lifetime hideaway, a sanctuary from unfinished life stories, stuffed in a personal back drawer awaiting the resolution of a final chapter. Slim filled that profile, living at the stable that had served as his retreat for over fifteen years. Well into his fifties, he possessed a long-faded Tom Selleck handsomeness of which he seemed totally unaware. He kept himself and his story private, communicating more through his hands to the horses in his care than to the riders he legged easily up into the saddle.

Carly was one of those riders, exercising sale horses while on a break from college. She had been a student of the stable since her first walk-trot lesson at age seven. As long as she could remember, tall, lanky Slim had been a fixture as head groom in Aisle 2. In her early years as a student riding the school horses stabled in Aisle 3, she had not had any cross-aisle exposure to Slim. However, now elevated to exercise girl status of the sale horses in Aisle 2, Slim was her first line of contact with the horses she rode.

While all four of the stable's aisles were neatly maintained under the supervision of their respective grooms, Aisle 2 was the model of efficiency. Slim ran it and the horses in his charge with military precision. Everything, no matter how small, was assigned a tidy place. Woe be unto anyone failing to return a piece of equipment to its designated location.

Although the stable didn't have a strict dress code for grooms beyond tidiness, Slim presented himself with the same professional demeanor as his aisle. He was always attired in a denim work shirt tucked into khaki pants – a bit frayed around the hem, but always clean to start off the day. He kept his graying hair neatly trimmed, never letting it get long enough to straggle over the collar.

Each morning he was given an order of go from the head trainer. It was Slim's responsibility to prep the horses, then hand the reins over to Carly. Even though they were usually just schooling sessions for the trainer's eyes only, each horse was meticulously turned out to Slim's exacting standards as though being prepped for a potential buyer. Not a speck of shavings ever clung to luxurious tails or dirt could be found smudged on braided reins. At the end of each schooling session, Carly would return to Aisle 2 to exchange mounts with Slim, who would put up the worked horse with the same scrupulous care with which he had been prepared.

Six days a week they worked in quiet harmony, prepping and exercising the stable's string of sale horses under the trainer's guiding eye. In Aisle 2, they rarely conversed except when Carly had to convey the trainer's instructions concerning adjustments to the care of the horses. Slim was always attentive to her message, but rarely communicated more than an acknowledging nod as he led the horse off to fulfill the instruction.

He seemed perfectly self-contained, never reaching out to the other grooms or clients on any personal matters. The stable community respected his unspoken request to honor the invisible walls he had erected to insulate his life. Like everyone else, Carly acquiesced to his wishes, but was ever-so-curious to cross over the line just to know him a little better.

One afternoon when the work was finished and all the horses had been put up, she decided to question the trainer, but he could add little dimension to the mystery that was Slim. "He's been with me for over fifteen years. Came here with all the talent you see today. I don't know where he learned it, but he's the best groom I've ever run across. As you've seen, he has a natural calming influence on all the horses, especially the green ones. Really has a knack of getting inside their heads. On top of that, he knows medications and treatments as well as most vets."

Carly nodded in agreement. "I've learned so much from him, but I just wish he'd let me in a little. We work together every day, but I still don't know anything about him outside the barn aisle. What does he like besides the horses? Where's he from? Any family? Even something as basic as favorite movies. All the everyday stuff you usually share with the person you work with. But whenever I start to broach any subject that doesn't relate to the horses, he breaks eye contact and moves away."

"He's a very good man, but there's certainly some deep water there," the trainer agreed. "Don't take it personally, Carly. He's always been that way with everyone. Not what you'd call unfriendly, just very distant.

"I don't know much more than you do about his personal life," he continued, "but he's proven his worth and loyalty to this stable time and time again. When it comes to where it counts most with the horses, there's no one better. Never asks for extra time off. Happy to live here 24/7. In fact, next week is the first time in three years that he's asked for a long weekend off."

+++++++++

11

Friday morning, Slim made one final pass down Aisle 2 to be certain everything was in order before leaving for the weekend. The big chestnut in the second stall nickered to attract his attention. He paused to gently stroke the white snip on the nose of the horse that was his favorite.

When Carly came into the aisle, she found Slim still in front of the stall, lost in deep thought. His left hand continued to stroke the chestnut while his right rested on the stall bars. As she approached, she noticed a ring on his right hand that she had never seen before. It was an ornate gold band set with a large amethyst encircled by lettering that she couldn't make out.

She definitely had to do a double-take, as Slim was totally transformed. Dressed in a navy blazer with white button-down shirt, he wore new khakis with a deep, clean press and unfrayed hems. He had even replaced his scuffed, cap-toed work boots with shiny black leather tassel loafers. He reminded her far more of a prospective client than the groom she worked beside every day.

"Wow, aren't you sharp!" she exclaimed. "You really clean up well!"

Slim turned, startled by the unexpected company. Instinctively, his left hand reached across to cover the ring on his right hand.

"Just finishing a final stall check, then I'm on my way," he replied cautiously.

Maybe it was the new clothes or the fact that for the first time she had caught him with his guard down, but there was definitely a different aura about him. She sensed he might be more approachable, as though his usually guarded personal door had opened just a crack.

Carly was determined to slip through that crack as far as she could while the opportunity existed. "Where are you off to, all duded up? Must be someplace really special. Big weekend plans?"

Slim turned to leave without answering, but then hesitated at the door, looking back at her as if a part of him was tempted to reach out, if only for a moment. He radiated an undercurrent of excitement and what hinted at pride that he had never before revealed to her.

"Guess it is a pretty special weekend," he admitted, fingering the ring on his right hand. "I'm heading up to West Point. So I better get on the road. It's a long drive."

Carly couldn't have been more astonished. "West Point? Whatever for?"

Slim paused, then flashed a wide smile. "My son's graduating this weekend."

13

"Your son?" Carly was totally taken aback. Not only did this loner whom she had always considered without family have a grown son, but that son was about to graduate from the venerable West Point.

"He's a very special kid," Slim said fondly. "Even graduating with honors."

"But West Point!" Carly exclaimed. "That's amazing. I mean really terrific! Why don't you ever talk about him? None of us at the stable even knew you had a son, let alone a West Point cadet."

Slim shrugged, continuing to twist his ring. "Not much to talk about now. Some things in the past are best left in the past. But still, this is a special day to celebrate an exceptional kid. Guess it proves after all that he wanted to follow in his old man's footsteps … at least part of them."

Carly was puzzled. "Follow in your footsteps? But you just said he's graduating from West Point. That can't mean he wants to work with horses."

Slim smiled a crooked smile and then hesitantly extended his right hand towards her. Curious, Carly looked down, finally able to read the inscription around the amethyst stone. To her total amazement, it read "West Point 1971."

After learning he had a son graduating from the army academy, she thought nothing could have surprised her more, but the ring topped it. "You went to West Point?" she whispered in awe.

He solemnly nodded. "Family tradition. My son's the fourth generation to graduate. So I need to be there this weekend to salute him."

"But, what about ..." Carly started to ask, but he cut her off.

Slim gently placed his long index finger to her lips. "Enough said. Some things are best left alone. And I appreciate you not sharing this conversation. No one else here needs to know the details of this weekend. It would just lead to a lot of questions and speculation that I don't have the time or inclination to answer. Let's just keep this information between us and not speak of it again. Okay?"

He winked as he stepped back, brushing off his jacket sleeve where it had gathered a speck of barn dust. "Take good care of my horses while I'm away. See you Monday. Eight o'clock sharp."

Without another word, he turned and walked briskly out of the aisle, head erect and shoulders square. Carly regretfully sensed it signaled his veil of privacy dropping between them again. Much as her curiosity had been piqued, she knew she had to respect his request. However, she would forever remember the tantalizing moment when she had been invited to peek behind the curtain – if only for a moment – of the man who ruled Aisle 2.

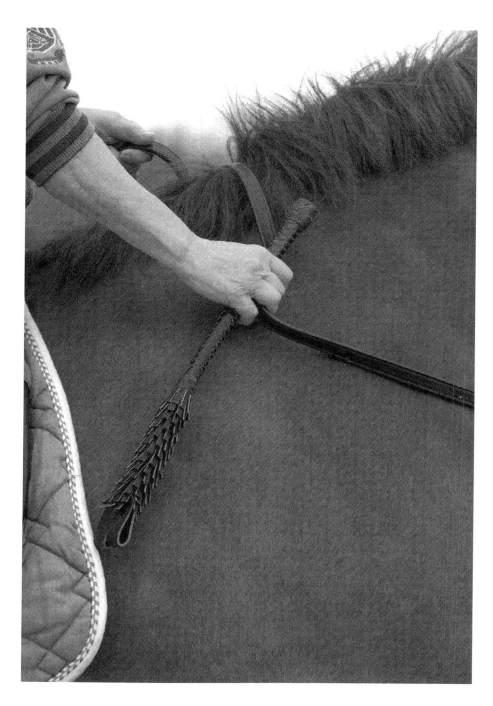

CHAPTER TWO
NATALIE'S HANDS

S ally's mother was a model in the 1950s. Not the ultra-glam, strut-your-stuff runway bustier-with-wings variety, but a sophisticated hand model at Marshall Fields in Chicago. Jill was employed to display jewelry and gloves on her delicate hands to shoppers visiting the downtown store. Outfitted in the latest fashions supplied by the ladies suit department, she would casually stroll through the store carrying a discreet sign in her left hand that let shoppers know where they could purchase the merchandise that adorned her body.

Jill had mastered her craft at the Patricia Stevens Charm School, a two-decades-old institution dedicated to instilling grace and etiquette to upwardly mobile young women. Exceeding the school's high expectations, upon graduation she had been offered a position on the instructional staff. When Sally came into her life, Jill made it her mission to mold her daughter into the same image of buffed nails, coiffed dos and social graces that would make "Miss Manners" proud.

Jill's work at the school, as well as at the department store, required a special style that set her apart from most of Sally's friends' pedal pusher, stay-at-home moms. Her mother never left the house without being turned out in matching twin set topping a coordinated skirt or pressed slacks. Sally couldn't ever recall her ever owning a pair of jeans. But she never felt it was her mother's motivation to show off; it was just her personal code from which she refused to stray.

Most memorable to anyone who met Jill were her delicate hands with the long, graceful fingers, each nail always painted a perfect, chip-free red. She took meticulous care, soaking them each night in conditioners and rubbing with nourishing oils to keep them baby soft. At the end of the ritual, she would cover them with a pair of soft white cotton gloves that were worn to bed.

"These hands are my stock-in-trade," she would explain whenever Sally watched her nightly routine. "You have to take special care of the things that are important to you if you want them to last."

Like all young girls born in the mold of their mother's inspiration, in the early years Sally honestly tried to please and be the daughter Jill envisioned. In fact, it wasn't that hard, spurred on by the envy of her school buddies who thought Jill's special style set her apart as the "coolest" mom on the block.

At eight, Sally was well on her way to fulfilling Jill's aspirations. She had even learned her mother's professional model's walk, head held high, balancing a book across the living room floor, proper pivot turn, then back without an embarrassing drop. That spring, Sally joined her in the annual "mother-daughter" tea room fashion show at Marshall Fields. Sally wore a pale blue chiffon dress accented by a bright blue cummerbund bow that perfectly matched the intense blue of her mother's stylish tea dress. Holding Sally's small fingers in her perfectly-manicured hand, Jill proudly led her down the runway for the first time, enjoying the flattering comments made by the audience digesting the show with their coffee and cakes.

All Jill's carefully laid plans seemed to be falling into place until the first Saturday in June in the summer of Sally's ninth year. Although it diverged entirely from the life itinerary she had always envisioned for her daughter, Jill had finally relented to Sally's persistent begging to take riding lessons. She was perplexed as to where Sally had caught the annoying horse obsession, but decided it was a small price to pay if a series of lessons were the cure to get her back on the planned journey that she had mapped out for her.

Despite Jill's attempt to ignore what she considered her daughter's affliction, Sally had been horse-crazed for as long as she could remember. No one in the family could understand her obsession with horses, as nobody else had ever personally experienced it. Sally's room was adorned with plush horses in all colors and sizes who shared her bedtime secrets. In her opinion, the next obvious step was to learn to ride a real live horse. It took a lot of creative convincing, but she had finally won the argument.

On the long-anticipated date, they drove down the stable's picturesque lane that bordered a large field set with colorful jumps. A handsome chestnut cantered boldly around the course, meeting each fence evenly with long strides. Mounted on his back was a graceful girl whose body seemed to mesh perfectly with the big horse. The rider leaned into his neck as they soared smoothly over each jump. Her hands followed his every movement, never getting in the way, never breaking the flow. It was flawless, as if the two were dance partners in perfect step. Even Jill, who had never been a horse lover, slowed the car to better appreciate the perfect pairing of woman and horse.

The first lesson was to be a private with one of the stable's instructors to assess her natural abilities and determine which class would be the best fit. Sally waited on the wooden bench beside the big indoor arena, proud of her shiny new jodhpurs and hard hat. She could barely contain her excitement as she watched a group of riders trot around the ring in front of her.

Hearing the clip-clop of approaching hooves on the concrete aisle, Sally turned to see a gentle-looking buckskin with a white star between two big, dark eyes. She was so thrilled to take in this beautiful creature who was about to be her first-ever ride that it took her a moment to recognize that the instructor leading him was the same woman she had watched jumping in the field.

While galloping around the course, the woman had seemed to assume the lanky chestnut's stature, but in reality, on the ground she was small and squarely built. Her dark hair was pulled back with a green ribbon into a short ponytail. She wore a navy polo shirt bearing the farm logo tucked into grey breeches smudged with dirt from a long day in the saddle.

She greeted Sally and Jill with a warm smile. "Welcome to the farm. I'm Natalie and this is Bucky. He's a great fellow; the very best and safest to introduce you to riding. I can't begin to tell you how many people he's started out. Now, let's get you up in the saddle, young lady."

As Natalie guided Bucky to the mounting block, Sally couldn't believe her luck that her first instructor was going to be the same amazing woman she had watched soar with perfection across the big field. As the instructor stood beside Bucky, showing her how to tighten the girth and adjust the stirrups, Sally was struck how the hands that were Natalie's stock-in-trade were so unlike her mother's.

By comparison, Natalie's hands were short and powerful. There was a dark bruise at the base of her right index finger. Large calluses marked the inside of the top knuckles of her ring fingers. Her nails were stubby and unpolished, with accumulated stable dirt packed around the cuticles. But as those strong, capable hands confidently helped Sally mount and settle into the saddle, she realized while they lacked physical beauty, they must possess a special magic to be able to pilot the beautiful chestnut so fluently around the jumps.

Natalie looked up with a smile as her hands closed around Sally's. Her fingers were warm and reassuring as they guided her to the proper way to hold the reins. Her grip exuded a confidence that went beyond words. In that moment, Sally was certain that these were the hands that she was really meant to have.

Although it would take time and patience, she was determined that one day she, too, would have hands that could soar effortlessly through the air with a horse; that one day, if she was lucky, she would have Natalie's hands.

CHAPTER THREE
THE DANCE

M argaret had been possessed from childhood by a burning horse fever that infected so many young girls obsessed with all things equine. Although never lucky enough to own a horse, she snatched every opportunity to ride. As luck would have it, there was a public stable within biking distance of her house. Birthday and Christmas gifts, as well as extra household chore money, all went toward treasured Saturday lessons. What Margaret lacked in natural athleticism she more than made up for in enthusiasm and courage, kicking on toward obstacles that defied many of her more talented classmates.

But as is the case of so many horse-crazed girls, as Margaret grew out of adolescence, she regretfully had to put her passion aside. While the horse fever never ceased to simmer beneath her surface, new priorities of work, marriage, and motherhood demanded her time and budget. Sadly, the cherished dream faded into the shadows of middle age, unfulfilled.

It wasn't until a mid-life move to Chicago that horses began to work their way back into Margaret's life. With her children grown and off building their own adult lives, she found herself with the luxury of personal freedom and discretionary income for the first time in twenty-five years. When a neighbor suggested she look into lessons at a nearby stable where her teenage daughter rode, Margaret decided it was definitely a sign to find her way back into the saddle.

Confidence buoyed by a tack shop spending spree, she headed to the stable for her first lesson in over two decades. Proudly dressed in new khaki-colored breeches and stiff black boots with a fresh out-of-the-box shine, she couldn't wait to step into the stirrups again. Unfortunately, the old adage that proper clothes do not necessarily make a proper rider proved true.

Once astride a plodding grey gelding, she was surprised by the overwhelming anxiety that suddenly gripped the pit of her stomach. She had to fight with every fiber of diminishing courage not to clutch the pommel of the saddle. Totally insecure, she was horrified to realize that all confidence had evaporated the moment her seat settled into the saddle. Aghast, she was faced with the harsh reality that her cherished memories of youthful daring had been unfairly supplanted by a moderately overweight, middle-aged woman in spotless new riding attire possessed of a passionate dream that lacked the courage to see it to fruition.

To Margaret, the instructor who held her trembling fate in her hands appeared barely older than the five teenagers who comprised the rest of the class. While the girl may have been a good cheerleader for the others who were nearly her peers, she lacked the skills to instill confidence in a frightened woman easily old enough to be her mother. At the end of the first lesson, it was a toss-up as to whether the instructor or Margaret was more frustrated with the lack of progress.

That evening, as Margaret studied her reflection in the bathroom mirror, she wondered what happened to that courageous girl who used to hurtle fearlessly across an open field at a breakneck gallop. Certainly the desire to ride still existed; in fact, she felt it burned even stronger from two decades of abstinence. However, despite all her desire, she couldn't ignore the crippling fear that overwhelmed her in the lesson. She wondered if its insidious presence grew from lack of doing, or perhaps fear of injury brought on by the self-doubts of middle age. Whereas to a child, a fall from a horse usually resulted in no more than an embarrassing tumble in the sand, to Margaret the mere thought seemed insurmountable.

Margaret loved horses too much to be defeated by this unfortunate initial setback, but she was wise enough to realize that to continue she would require a more experienced trainer who understood that her needs differed from a teenager's fearless enthusiasm. Thus began a string of stables and resultant disappointments in Margaret's quest to find the consummate instructor who could help her rediscover the confidence necessary to quench her equine thirst.

While searching for the ideal instructor, a friend invited her to attend a summer performance of the Lipizzans of Tempel Farms in Old Mill Creek, a mere forty-five-minute drive north of the city. The afternoon excursion promised a delightful afternoon in the country, watching magnificent white stallions performing true classical dressage to choreographed music.

The promotional flyer Margaret received explained that Tempel Farms had been founded in 1958 by Chicago industrialist Tempel Smith, who launched his program with twenty purebred Lipizzans imported from the Austrian state stud in Piber. He had carefully built his stable to become the largest privately-owned herd of Lipizzans in the world.

Following in the venerated traditions of the Spanish Riding School in Vienna, Tempel Farms established an American center for classical dressage, performing nationwide from major area venues to White House inaugurals.

Margaret was thrilled to receive the invitation. She had long been a fan of the beautiful breed that was considered the horse of the Renaissance. A little research informed her that Lipizzans had originally been protected by royalty. The first stud was established in Lipizza in 1580 by Austrian Archduke Charles II. Due to the unsettled political nature of the area ,the breed led a tenuous existence. During the Napoleonic Wars, the State Stud was forced to move three times. By the end of World War I, only 208 purebred Lipizzans existed in the world.

As Margaret learned, World War II presented the breed with yet another crisis that necessitated evacuation from their home location to avoid the advancing Russian army. Only unprecedented action by U.S. General George S. Patton was responsible for saving the Lipizzans' unique bloodlines. The story of General Patton and his Second Cavalry Division's protection of the herd from certain extinction was made famous in 1963 by the Disney movie *Miracle of the White Stallions*. The movie had been Margaret's childhood favorite, so when the opportunity arose to attend a live performance of the revered horses, she eagerly accepted.

On the appointed day, Margaret and her friend took centerline seats in the Tempel Farms' bleachers. The sell-out crowd surrounded a pristine sand rectangle rimmed by a short white board perimeter. From the moment the horses entered the arena, Margaret was captivated by the performance. The show presented the progressive development of Lipizzans from farm-bred youngsters exhibited in-hand to the highest levels of classical dressage including the airs above the ground.

The magnificent horses were mounted by elegant riders attired in traditional hats and bright navy double-breasted tail coats highlighted by red collar and cuffs. Their shiny black boots extended several inches above the knee of white breeches. Under each saddle was a bright red pad that provided striking contrast to the horses' glistening white coats. From the thrilling performance choreographed to music to the announcer's commentary of the breed's unique history, Margaret was hooked.

During intermission, the woman sitting next to her spoke up. "I couldn't help but notice how much you're enjoying the performance. Is this your first time seeing the Lipizzans?"

Margaret grinned sheepishly. "Guess it was pretty obvious. I feel just like a kid in a candy store. I've always admired this breed through pictures and movies, but I had no idea how truly magnificent they were until seeing them in person today."

The woman nodded, brushing back a graying strand of hair from her forehead. "I agree, but I've seen them so many times that it was fun to get a fresh perspective through your eyes. By the way, my name is Christine."

"Margaret," she replied, extending her hand. "And this is my friend, Joan, who was so nice to invite me to this wonderful performance. It must be an incredible experience to ride one of those magnificent horses."

"It truly is," Christine assured her. "I used to ride in the show when I was younger, but now I've got my own farm and training business a few miles down the road. I still keep in touch with old friends here and come to watch whenever they introduce new horses to the show, like the two young geldings in the second act."

It was impossible for Margaret to keep the awe out of her voice. "You've actually ridden in these shows?"

Christine smiled. "I was fortunate to be part of this at one time. It's a very special memory. Are you a rider?"

Margaret sadly shrugged. "Not sure of the answer to that question. I'd like to say yes, but think I'm better classified as a 'wannabe.' I rode as a kid and loved it, but one thing, then another, kept me out of the saddle until last year. Now that I finally have the opportunity to ride again, I haven't had any luck finding the right instructor," she continued, frustration evident in her voice. "The old love and desire are strong as ever, but my skill sets and confidence are totally gone. All the instructors I've tried are so young and impatient. They just don't seem to realize what I'm going through every time I step in the stirrups."

"I totally understand," Christine sympathized. "I hear that from a lot of middle-aged women who've never ridden or are getting back on after years out of the saddle. It's just not the same looking down from sixteen hands at fifty as it was when you were fifteen."

"Exactly!" Margaret exclaimed. "But try as I might, I haven't been able to find an instructor who understands my dilemma."

Christine pulled a business card out of her jeans. "My farm may be a bit of a drive from the city, but I think my training system can help you work through your confidence predicament."

Looking down at the card that read "Forever Fields," Margaret felt a glimmer of hope. "I will definitely give you a call next week."

Christine redirected their attention to the warm-up arena behind the presentation ring. "Watch what's coming next. They're about to do the Quadrille. That was always my favorite ride."

"Isn't that a group of four?" Margaret asked.

"Exactly, but it has such a rich history," Christine explained. "Riding quadrilles originated in the mid-1700s in French military parades where four horsemen and their mounts performed square-shaped formations. The techniques of quadrille riding have origins in the training centers of Saumur, France, and the Spanish Riding School in Vienna that practiced military tactics including formation riding. Mounted battles at that time were fought in linear formations that required horsemen to execute maneuvers in perfect harmony at the same tempo. The ability to move as one was of utmost importance on the battlefield. The demanding precision has translated to what you'll see in the performance today."

She nodded proudly toward the four elegantly-attired riders who rode head-to-tail into the arena, slowly doffing their hats to salute the crowd in perfect unison. "Just sit back and enjoy."

The riders circled the arena half-passing, cantering, and piaffing in perfect mirror image harmony to the strains of Vivaldi's "Four Seasons" that filled the arena. At the end of the flawless performance, Margaret was one of the first to jump to her feet with the applause, overcome by the dream that some way, somehow, she would love to experience that dance.

When the performance concluded, Christine waved goodbye, leaving the stands to catch up with the riders at the far end of the arena. Margaret thoughtfully turned over the business card, thinking that maybe, just maybe, it could be her ticket into this magical world.

As the weeks passed, Margaret quickly learned that Christine had been correct about the long commute from Chicago to the cozy training barn tucked into the rolling Wadsworth hills. But for Margaret, the investment in travel time proved well worth the drive. In Christine and her dependable black lesson mare, she finally found the confidence she had had been seeking. Once Margaret was willing to admit that the bravado of her youth would never be more than a long-past memory and that a rolling canter would probably always remain a breath-holding bugaboo, lessons became anticipations of eager joy rather than uncertain dread.

Under Christine's patient tutelage, Margaret made steady progress in the saddle. Weekly lessons expanded to two that led to a half-lease on a retired show Connemara named Buster who was owned by one of the boarders. He proved to be a perfect walk-trot partner whose canter had faded away with the stiffening arthritis of age.

As an unexpected bonus, not only did Christine prove to be the ideal instructor, she also became Margaret's backstage pass for the magic of the neighboring Tempel Lipizzans. As a retired Tempel rider and still-devoted supporter, Christine was always a welcome visitor to the farm. Aware of Margaret's passionate love for the breed, Christine was happy to let her tag along on visits. Much to Margaret's delight, it wasn't long before she became first-name acquaintances with many of the riders she had originally admired from afar.

On the day of Margaret's milestone sixtieth birthday, Christine posed the question that had been growing in both their minds. "It's about time for Buster to fully retire. We can find you another suitable lease, but why don't you finally treat yourself to your own horse? You're more than ready."

"I've been thinking the same thing lately," Margaret admitted. "But where would we ever find one as patient as Buster?"

Christine gave her a knowing wink. "I have a friend I want you to meet who just may have the perfect solution. Hop in the car."

Ever the willing pawn for Christine's contagious enthusiasm, Margaret slipped into the passenger seat of the Land Rover without hesitation, unable to guess their destination. Much to her surprise, a few miles down the road they turned into the Tempel Farms' drive.

Christine had Margaret wait beside the entrance to the big indoor arena while she slipped into the stable. A few minutes later she returned leading a handsome white Lipizzan gelding tacked up to be ridden. His hoofs rang out down the concrete aisle as he walked companionably along, rubbing her shoulder with his big head.

Christine stopped beside Margaret, extending the reins with a smile. "Meet my dear friend, Alma. He was my partner years ago when I rode in the Quadrille. He's twenty-two now and retired from the program, but still totally sound and the kindest, safest horse you'll ever meet. I know he'd love nothing more than to help you celebrate your birthday, so how about a ride?"

As Margaret reached out in disbelief to stroke the soft hair of his neck, he gave her a playful butt with his nose. In all her visits admiring the beautiful horses of

Tempel Farms, she had never imagined she would have the opportunity to actually ride one.

"What a perfect birthday gift!" she exclaimed as Christine led Alma to the mounting block. "Thank you so much!"

From the moment she sat atop the gelding, Margaret was enthralled by the view from the saddle. She shivered with goose bumps just looking over the powerful white neck through his small ears that pricked just for her. She ran her fingers across his slick neck, hardly daring to believe her luck.

The ride flew by, with Christine coaching Margaret through movements she had never imagined experiencing. Alma's broad back swung softly beneath her, perfectly filling up her legs. Every aspect of the ride inspired her with an unexpected confidence to sit proudly erect. Some of the Tempel riders she knew even stopped ringside to watch and give supportive thumbs up. At the end of the ride, Christine walked beside the horse, making little clucking sounds. Alma immediately responded, stepping obediently into an elegant piaffe followed by a square, immobile halt.

Margaret joyfully threw her arms around his neck. "Oh, you perfectly wonderful creature. Thank you! Thank you!"

Christine grinned with pride at the pleasure her treasured old partner had brought to her new friend. "So, what do you think of Alma?"

"He's a total dream!" Margaret exclaimed. "I never imagined I could actually ride like that on a horse like this. Thank you so much, Christine. This is the best birthday gift ever!"

Christine stroked the horse's neck as he affectionately rubbed his cheek against her back. "Alma's very special. We have a lot of history. I've missed riding the old bugger, but last week I had an inspiration. The barn manager told me the farm needs to cut expenses, so they're looking for homes for some of the retired herd. You and Alma are obviously a perfect match. So I think he's the birthday gift you should give yourself. What do you say?"

Margaret caught her breath, barely able to process all that was happening. But for once she didn't second-guess herself or the incredible opportunity that Christine was making possible. In that spontaneous moment, she joyfully agreed to give herself the wonderful gift of Alma.

True to Christine's prediction, they were a perfect match right from the beginning. The dependable senior gelding became Margaret's ideal partner; never too quick, never impatient, never spooky. He was content to shoulder her insecurities and cruise along in her comfort zone. When the canter still gave her cause to stress, he was just as happy to trot, offering a little piaffe or passage that made her laugh with delight if she closed her legs and the reins in just the right way.

Each ride was magical, filling her head with lyrical music that she happily hummed as they circled the arena. Her enthusiasm reawakened the retired gelding's joy as he, too, seemed to again hear the music that had defined his youth and long-past performance career.

Every time Margaret mounted, Alma willingly shared more and more of his story, taking her on a journey she had never imagined possible. With each ride, they became more in tune to the music she softly hummed to her handsome baroque partner. His broad, confident back effortlessly released her from the fear and frustration that had so long held her prisoner as he swept her across the sand of his dance floor, making all her Cinderella dreams come true.

CHAPTER FOUR
SIMPLY THE BEST

W hat force of nature exposes us to opportunity and those life-altering choices that tempt with promise? Is it fate or circumstance – or could it be just plain luck? Do we notice the moment when fortune taps us on the shoulder? Or are we predestined to be in a specific place at a specific time like star-crossed lovers?

No matter the cause, when Anne first saw the chestnut gelding, the thought of adding a green broken three-year-old to her life was not even a figment of her imagination. She was comfortably traversing middle age on the back of a patient fourteen-year-old dressage schoolmaster without any desire or inclination to revisit the bumps and grinds of the fractious youngsters who had filled the years of her youth.

She and her husband were on vacation in Maryland, visiting good friends to catch up on old times and admire their latest crop of imported Warmbloods. Even though she assured her husband as well as herself that she wasn't horse shopping, it only made sense to pack boots and breeches. After all, they were traveling to horse heaven, so it would never do to arrive unprepared. But honestly, her plan was just to "ooh" and "aah" over some elegant young Swedish Warmblood prospects, then retreat to a favorite crab shack to enjoy the Chesapeake's finest along with the camaraderie of longtime friends.

Anne certainly hadn't made the trip East in search of a strapping young chestnut barely six weeks under saddle who was only just beginning to find the answers to the questions posed by the humans who governed his life. But from her first steps down their friends' barn aisle, that colt with the long white blaze fixated his attention on her and never let go. He hung his beautiful head over the Dutch door, following her every movement even before their first introduction at his stall. Whenever she was within eyeshot, she felt his penetrating, inviting gaze as though impatiently waiting for her to discover what he already appeared to know.

She politely professed interest in all of the talented new prospects as they were trotted out into the arena for show. Focusing on the glistening group of youngsters, she tried to keep her interest in the handsome chestnut casual. But despite Anne's best efforts, it was impossible for anyone to miss their flirtation.

Ever the horse dealer, her friend was quick to produce tack with a casual encouragement of, "Special, isn't he? Why don't you hop on? Just for fun."

Initially, Anne hesitated, responsibly restrained by budget and the time constraints of her stable at home. However, there was no denying that she was more than curious to explore the tantalizing potential of the relationship offered by the colt. With a supportive nod from her husband, there was nothing left to do but take the reins and see where they led.

Where Anne had expected to feel the usual uncertainty and imbalance of the many newly-broken horses she had ridden over the years, beneath her seat she was delighted to discover a raw confidence and power emanating from gaits that hinted of all the potential yet to be revealed. Despite his youth, he gave her the steady assurance of undaunted courage, especially evident when a gaggle of geese soared overhead to land very much uninvited in the center of the outdoor arena during their ride.

She was amazed that he could be so unflappable at such a young age. He seemed to know exactly what she needed in her life, when before that weekend she hadn't even known herself. When Anne dismounted at the end of the ride, she was certain in her heart that before she headed home she would have no choice but to make arrangements for this new, unexpected chestnut man in her life to follow in short order.

But even as Anne made that momentous decision, she wondered if there was a litmus test to determine the potential merits of this prospect who she hoped would carry her to the fulfillment of the unspoken dreams she still kept tucked privately away. Could her spontaneous actions be dictated by a law of nature that ordained all the pieces and parts of this adventure would ultimately mesh into a perfect whole for her and this particular horse?

Anne realized that this youngster represented an untested gamble on potential that entwined bloodlines, conformation, and purity of gaits with the vision of her long-pursued dream. She knew that in many disciplines the definitive payoff or disappointment comes early, as with Thoroughbreds who charge down the backstretch as two- and three-year-olds; careers often culminating before horses in many other disciplines are even broken to saddle. Experience had long ago taught her that the journey of the dressage horse was arguably the longest, measured in a training progression of years to achieve the ultimate peak rather than the limited competitive seasons of most show horses.

And so Anne vowed to begin a new journey *down the aisle* with this intriguing new partner, hoping against hope that he would be the one. As their training progressed, she introduced each new movement with the careful precision of a pianist composing a song, note by note, until the harmonies blended into a complete melody. Training, stretching, collecting, bending, extending together through the years, as one by one the questions of each progressive level were asked and successfully answered.

Together, Anne and the chestnut, who had selected her to be his partner that sunny summer day in Maryland, built layer upon layer of proficiency until only one hurdle remained. The day he answered that final question, something magical clicked and they soared to a new height, discovering the final groove of engagement that lifted them effortlessly around the arena in a rhythmic passage. With each stride, his pride and confidence swelled, elevating them to that special place that had beseeched Anne from the eyes of a green-broken three-year-old eight long years ago.

+++++++++++

Each year, Anne and her husband's annual farm Christmas gift to their horse friends was a custom-made CD. Everyone was invited to submit the song whose lyrics they felt best represented their goals and vision for the year ahead with their favorite horse. Imaginations were set free, guaranteeing the creation of a truly unique recording that set the tone for the upcoming year for everyone on the farm team. From "Don't Worry Be Happy" to "With a Little Help from My Friends" to "True Colors," it was a gift that everyone enjoyed receiving to play throughout the new season.

Anne's selection that year could have served as her chestnut's theme song, ever since their first auspicious meeting so many years ago at her friends' farm in Maryland. But somehow his mastery of the final piece of the Grand Prix made it all the more appropriate for the big devoted gelding whose total focus had never wavered whenever she was within his eyeshot. Without hesitation, she chose the Tina Turner classic "Simply the Best", because in her eyes and heart he was, and always would be.

CHAPTER FIVE
THE SIGN

A small red bus waited with engine running in front of the grey brick stable entrance. A long-established arch of ivy grew over the open double doors fronted by black cast iron pots of geraniums. Beyond the doors stretched two long aisles of stalls with Dutch windows overlooking big pastures.

The bus driver honked the horn. In response, nine chattering children dressed in boots and breeches ran out of the barn to scramble aboard. After waiting a few minutes, the driver sounded the horn again followed by a third longer, demanding blare. Finally, a small girl with long brown braids scurried out of the stable toward the bus.

A silver-haired man impeccably dressed in tall boots and flared cavalry twill breeches topped by a grey hacking jacket stood at the edge of the outdoor arena watching her with an amused smile. "Birdie," he called in a voice tinged with a German accent. "Why is it always you the bus must wait for, my cute girl?"

She scrunched up her freckled nose and shrugged as she climbed the bus steps. "Sorry, Captain, but Co-Co had a really big itch. I mean I just couldn't leave until I helped him scratch it. See you next week!"

He shook his head with a laugh, waving Birdie and the other students on their way. The bus turned left out of the stable yard, passing a large white entrance sign that advertised "Captain Ritter's Academy" flanked by two black silhouetted jumping horses.

When the bus had disappeared from sight, the Captain returned his attention back to the farm. He fondly gazed beyond the stable to the outdoor arena filled with brightly-painted fences where his life had been centered for the past forty years. Behind the arena stretched a rolling pasture where two chestnut Hanoverian mares amicably grazed side by side. Even from a distance, he could see their bellies swollen with the spring foals soon to be delivered.

The Captain drew his bushy eyebrows together with a sigh at the sight that was ever reminiscent, yet so far removed, from a long-ago broodmare pasture where in 1937, on the left bank of the River Leine not far from the outskirts of Hanover, there had stood another sprawling horse farm. It had been anchored by a sturdy, two-storey stone house framed by blue shutters that shared a cobblestone courtyard with a weathered stone stable. Beyond the barn and outdoor training arena had stretched lush pastures populated by shiny mares and their foals.

On a tall stone gate post at the head of the long farm lane hung a handcrafted wooden sign. To all visitors, it identified the property as "Hoff Ritter," carefully lettered above a carved "H" that was the Hanoverian breed brand symbol. For four generations, the sign had been lovingly maintained by a family proud of their heritage and the fine horses they bred.

The elite mares of Hoff Ritter had the luxury of convenient access to the select Hanoverian stallions standing nearby at the State Stud of Celle. The venerable Stud was established on July 27, 1735, by George II, King of England and Elector of Hanover. Created with the intent to improve the quality of local bloodstock, the Crown had sought to develop regionally superior horses in order to reduce the need of importing them from England in times of war.

Steeped in the German equestrian tradition, the Ritter family was proud of their distinguished cavalry connections. The firstborn of each Hoff Ritter generation followed his father's service to the military without question. Successive sons and daughters remained at home, dedicated to the continuation of breeding quality Hanoverian horses to serve their country.

Twenty-year-old Markus Ritter was honored to be accepted into the Military Riding Institute of Hanover. Only the most exceptional officer candidates were invited to attend the intensive two-year training program. He entered the school mounted on his favorite homebred, Regent. He had been closely connected to the gelding since assisting in his difficult foaling four years earlier. The striking black horse with two matching hind socks was equally devoted to his master, who had managed every step of his breaking and training.

Markus graduated with honors from the Institute in August, 1939, on the eve of World War II. He was one of the first to be commissioned as a captain into the German 1st Cavalry Division, newly-formed that October. Garrisoned in Insterburg, they proudly wore the insignia of a jumping horse to honor the legacy of their mounted predecessors. They swore to the motto of the German cavalry, which was "Das paradies der erde lieght aug den rucken der pferda," translated to "Paradise on earth is on the backs of horses."

While the majority of the British mounted regiments were mechanized prior to the outbreak of

World War II, the German cavalry increased from a single brigade to six divisions by 1945. At the beginning of the war, the German army had 524,000 horses and mules, but their numbers swelled to 2.75 million by war's end. While the majority of the horses were assigned to pull artillery, each infantry division maintained a reconnaissance battalion of 216 cavalrymen.

Due to limited fuel resources, horses provided an important source of troop and equipment transportation. Unaffected by those shortages, they could even be counted on to survive off the land when hay was not available. They could also carry soldiers across the extreme terrain conditions of the Balkan Mountains and the trackless wastes of eastern Russia.

Markus and Regent were assigned to head up a reconnaissance division on the Eastern Front. It was a brutal mission, riding through the harshest weather over land that was often impassable for the infantry and mechanized divisions. He was on a rapid learning curve since joining the division, quickly realizing that the skills required of an elite trained cavalry officer on the battlefield did not include knowing how to read the strides to a tricky triple combination or maintaining the tight formation grouping of a mock charge.

But through all the danger and deprivation, Markus and Regent's devotion to each other never faltered. Even as comrades and their mounts fell around them under the relentless barrage of enemy fire, their partnership strengthened as they fought under seemingly impossible odds. In one particularly brutal skirmish, Markus was seriously wounded in his side. As he slumped forward over the saddle, struggling to maintain consciousness, Regent swayed beneath his unstable rider to prevent him from falling in the mud. In that moment of imbalance, the brave gelding took a bullet in the base of his neck. He struck out, screaming at the sudden, burning pain. But never once did he falter beneath his master. The courageous gelding safely carried Markus back behind friendly lines where they were both treated for their wounds, returning together to fight on until the war finally drew to a close.

In the final months of the war, outside communication with family and friends broke down in the chaos of a losing effort. Markus had not received any concrete news of his parents' circumstances in nearly five months. Two years earlier, he had mourned the loss of his younger brother, who had been drafted into the German 6th Army only to lose his life in the battle of Kursk on the Russian front.

Despite the mounting horror stories from all sides, Markus refused to lose faith, praying that the rest of his family remained safe on their home farm. He clung desperately to their precious memory that he held close to his heart on bleak, frigid nights, like the worn picture of his parents that was always buttoned into the breast pocket of his shirt.

After enduring the harsh deprivations of war for six long years, Markus was finally released to begin the long ride home on Regent. They found themselves one among many amidst the straggling stream of war-weary soldiers and refugees crowding the roadways. Riding slowly west, he sadly surveyed the seemingly endless damage to his homeland, overwhelmed by the near total devastation to the once-verdant farmland and vibrant cities.

However, nothing could have prepared him for the horrific sights as he and Regent wove their way through the bomb craters that pockmarked the approach to the outskirts of Hanover. His once-proud home city that had been an important railroad junction and bustling manufacturing center in northern Germany had become a strategic bombing target of the Allies, who had all but leveled its primary locations.

Overwhelmed by an uneasy sense of urgency, Markus urged Regent forward without pausing in the city. Despite the urban devastation that stretched in all directions, he prayed it hadn't extended to his family's home nestled in a peaceful bend in the River Leine well beyond the city's manufacturing center.

A mile from home, he stopped in front of a neighbor's farm. Old Mrs. Krause had been his mother's dearest friend, sharing everything from the births of their children to the physical trials of raising them in the country. Everything from triumphs to tragedies had been carried companionably on the two women's shoulders.

As Markus approached the farm, he noticed that part of the roof of the sturdy old stone house had collapsed. In its place was a battered tarp, haphazardly draped over the rafters to keep out the weather. Although the dairy barn beside the house still appeared intact, there was no sign of the cows Mrs. Krause had so proudly tended for as long as he could remember.

Wearing a tattered brown plaid dress, Mrs. Krause slumped on the stoop of what remained of her war-damaged home. Elbows propped on her knees, she held her head in her hands, unaware of Markus' approach. When he stopped Regent in front of the house, she finally looked up with a sad smile of recognition without making any attempt to rise.

"Dear Markus," she sighed, her voice a weary rasp. "So you have made it back safely. My sweet boy, it is good to meet a face that I did not expect to ever see again. When there was no news for so many months, I worried perhaps you had met with the same end as your brother and my poor son, Dieter. Only Fritz is left now. He does what he can, but there is so little left for anyone."

"Oh no, not Dieter," Markus moaned with dismay at the loss of yet another of his close childhood friends.

The hint of tears on the woman's cheeks brought tears to his own eyes. He quickly swung out of the saddle to sit beside her on the stoop. When he draped a comforting arm around her thin shoulders, she sank gratefully into his touch. For a long moment, they huddled in silence on the memory of their losses.

Markus hesitated, barely daring to pursue the fate of his family. "But what news of my mother and father? And my sisters, Brigitta and Sophie? I've had no word from home for months since communication at the front broke down."

Mrs. Krause drew back to lovingly stroke his unshaven cheek. "Oh, dear Markus. You don't have any idea, do you?"

In response to the dread in his eyes, she stood and gently took his hand. "Come in the house. There is much to tell. It will be easier to hear over a little schnapps. I still have some tucked away for important times."

She offered him one of the three remaining kitchen chairs, taking two blue chipped cups from the cabinet with the broken glass front. Filling the cups with schnapps, she raised her glass to him. "First, a toast to the blessed safe return of you and your beautiful Regent."

Then ever so tenderly as they drank, she began to relate the demise of life along the River Leine as it crumbled around the families who had considered it a safe home for generations. She explained that nearly six months earlier, the last of the wonderful Ritter horses had been requisitioned by the army for work – or an even worse fate too horrible to consider. Only an old broodmare had been left behind for the family's use on the farm. Although his father had born the disbandment of his prized herd in bitter silence, she was certain that his heart was broken, compounded by the loss of Franz and the uncertainty of Markus' fate.

"Not long after the first bombing raid on Hanover, he died in your farmyard of a heart attack," she gently concluded. "He was one of the strongest men I ever knew, but I think it was all just too much for him."

The shock of his father's unexpected death drained all the color from Markus' cheeks. As he slumped wordlessly back into his chair, Mrs. Kraus silently took his cold hands and warmed them between hers.

"Maybe it was best for him," she sadly consoled. "When the army robbed him of all his beautiful horses, they took his soul. After that day, he was only the shell of a broken man."

"And Mother?" Markus was finally able to whisper.

Mrs. Krause gave an uncertain shrug. "Marta, Brigitta, and Sophie survived the bombings, but there was nothing left for them at your farm. When the truck broke down months ago, there was no way to repair it. After that, they managed the best they could with the wagon and the old mare.

"Two months ago I helped them pack it up with the few things that could be salvaged from the farm," she continued. "Then they hitched up the old broodmare and headed for relatives near Bremen, I think."

She shook her head with a thin smile at the thought of her independent friend. "You know your mother, always the determined one."

As hope began to fill Markus' eyes, she was quick not to encourage. "I'm sad to say I haven't heard anything of them since they left. Between the bombings and all the starving refugees, the roads are not a safe place for three women traveling alone."

Markus pushed back his chair with sudden resolve. "I must go to the farm to see for myself."

Mrs. Krause took hold of his coat sleeve, trying to draw him back into the chair. "Please, Markus, stay awhile. This news is such a shock. You need to take some time. And truly, there is nothing to see any more."

With a soft kiss on the top of her head, Markus gently uncoiled the clasp of her fingers from his coat. "Dear Mrs. Krause, thank you for the schnapps and the comfort, but I must go see the farm for myself and then try to find the remains of my family."

However, even Mrs. Krause's dire warnings could not soften the shock as he rounded the bend in the river to catch his first glimpse of the abandoned ruins of his beloved family farm. All that remained was an unrecognizable burned-out shell of the house and barn, with broken pasture fence lines stretching beyond. Even the family dogs, who had never failed to trot up the lane with wagging tails to welcome visitors, were gone without a trace. It was almost impossible for him to process the scattered ruins that were yet another tragic collateral damage victim of the Allied bombings on Hanover.

Markus dismounted from Regent between the big stone gate posts that were the only standing visual reminder of the legacy that had been his ancestral home. Dangling askew from the right post hung the Hoff Ritter sign. It was still intact, except for a large crack that extended across the back.

He carefully lifted the sign from its last remaining nail. "This we take with us, Regent."

Pulling the stirrup leathers off the saddle, he buckled them together to make a strap long enough to hold the sign. Hooking the leathers around the cantle, he balanced the sign against the left side of the saddle. With a final bitter look back down the lane, he gathered Regent's reins and began the long walk toward Bremen.

Two days later, Markus happily reunited with his mother and sisters at their cousin's farm that had luckily survived the war intact. When he led Regent into the yard, they ran to him, stumbling over themselves with joy. Despite their elation, he immediately recognized the pain of the past years on their gaunt faces above worn clothes that hung loosely from their bodies. As they hugged and cried over each other, Markus vowed that going forward he would find a way to keep them forever safe, no matter what it took.

But as the world in which Markus was raised continued to crumble around them, it seemed everyone was desperately reaching out in any direction to grasp a hand-hold, no matter how tenuous by which to pull themselves and their families out of a near-certain abyss. With the cavalry disbanded, the war-shattered economy left few viable prospects for Markus' professional skills. As Germany had sorely suffered from the ravages of battle and the harsh sanctions imposed by the Allies at war's end, it would be many years before an income could again be earned training and breeding fine horses. The only work Markus could find were physical reconstruction jobs that barely paid a living wage for him, let alone provide for his mother and sisters.

The family reached out in all directions for help, no matter how remote. Finally, they were rewarded by a letter from his father's second cousin, Jurgen, who had immigrated to the United States in 1932. In the family tradition, he had opened a riding stable north of Milwaukee, where he built a thriving business.

At 55, he was getting up in years and in need of a skilled trainer to take his place starting the young prospects. Cousin Jurgen had been unable to find anyone in the States possessed of the traditional cavalry skills in which he had been trained. Well acquainted with Markus' background, he thought his kinsman would be a fine fit for the position. In exchange for work, he promised wages for training the horses, plus commissions for any sold. In addition, he would provide an apartment on the farm for Markus, who could also take his meals with Jurgen and his wife. As there would be no living expenses, Markus would have money to send home to his mother and sisters. Markus needed only to get himself to Milwaukee and the job would be his.

The proposition was the godsend for which the little family had been praying. But despite the opportunity, it also represented the final personal blow to Markus by a war that had stripped him of almost everything he had known and loved. Now in its aftermath, in order to move forward to rebuild and support his family, it demanded one final sacrifice.

The only way he could raise enough money to get to America was to sell his steadfast companion, Regent. The horse that had carried him safely through all the horrors of combat was his only possession of value. Even after the war, there were still some in Germany with the means to offer a generous price for a sound horse of Regent's quality and training. Such a horse was a much-sought-after rarity. His sale would provide the funds to pay for Markus' fare to America and the promise of real work that represented a future for his family. His only option was to place Regent in the best home he could find, then turn his hopes west toward the opportunity promised by cousin Jurgen.

While it broke his heart to part from his longtime treasured partner, Markus was grateful that Regent's new owner pledged to give him a quality life as a pleasure riding mount. Within only days of handing over the reins, Markus was on board a ship bound for the United States to begin the next chapter of his life.

Although initially in his new home Markus struggled to learn English, from the very start he fluently spoke the language of every horse he mounted. What he lacked in verbal skills was easily overcome in developing Jurgen's young jumper prospects. He also helped his cousin build a small band of quality broodmares. In time, they even managed to track down some of the bloodlines that had anchored the elite Hoff Ritter band in Germany.

Throughout the years, cousin Jurgen was more than good to his word. He proved to be a generous employer and trusted family member to guide Markus as he made his mark in America. Since Jurgen and his wife had no children of their own, he became totally devoted to Markus, who shared his passion for horses.

Jurgen became the ultimate benefactor at his death, entrusting his farm and business to Markus in the hope he would continue to develop the dream they had built together. It was the same dream that Captain Markus Ritter now saw fulfilled in the two pregnant broodmares amicably grazing in the big pasture before him.

Over his shoulder, he noticed the little red bus returning with a new group of students eager for their afternoon lesson. It slowly turned into the stable drive, passing the white Academy sign. Just below that sign hung a smaller, carefully hand painted sign that read "Hoff Ritter" above the "H" brand symbol of the Hanoverian breed. At first glance, it appeared the same age as the larger sign, but a closer inspection would reveal weathered edges and a long crack across the back that had been lovingly mended with a metal plate and eight screws.

CHAPTER SIX
HORSE SENSE

S erious horse professionals rarely have the good fortune to make a marital connection with an individual of similar ilk. In a perfect world, the logical life partner would link an equine-obsessive life with a kindred spirit. However, the "love conquers all/opposites attract" adage often overcomes common sense. In that case, it becomes the professional horsewoman's mission to attempt to immerse a non-riding spouse in a discipline that revolves around powerful, 1,200-pound creatures who are totally foreign and often understandably frightening to them.

Such was the case with Cindy's new husband, Joe. College sweethearts, followed by a two-year engagement, had more than revealed to him the dedication and sacrifice that a burgeoning horse training business required of an aspiring professional striving to make her mark in the industry. To his credit, Joe remained a perpetual good sport as Cindy strove to make a place for him in her equine-focused world where few non-riding retail store managers would have succeeded in securing a confident foothold.

Even if Joe didn't comfortably "ride the ride," through the early years of their developing relationship, he had definitely learned to "talk the talk." Hours of cheerleading Cindy and her students at horse shows, videotaping training sessions, as well as endless dinner table discussions had molded him into a competent sounding block. Although his skills were only verbal, he developed the proficient eye of an armchair quarterback who could be counted on to offer a valid appraisal at the end of a round. However, having a good feedback eye from the ground versus possessing the experience and horse sense to correct a problem under saddle was something he lost in translation.

Over their years together, Joe gradually began to show an interest in experiencing horses from their back as well as from the ground. Happy to help him make a positive transition into the saddle, Cindy initially matched him with her safest, slowest school horse. She even renamed the 15.1 hand, chunky buckskin gelding Roebuck, reasoning that if Joe's mount bore the name of his workplace, he would instinctively feel more at home in the saddle.

Her plan was an immediate success. Joe took the bait, investing in a pair of rough cowhide chaps, tooled black boots, and a brown felt hat onto which he added a long, mottled hawk tail feather tucked into the band. Even though his channeled cowboy spirit was slightly modified by the English saddle mode of transportation, he seemed content to join Cindy on ambling evening rides through the neighboring fields and woods, serenading her with off-key songs of the trail.

However, once Joe began to regularly throw a leg over the saddle without any negative repercussions from Roebuck, Cindy had a growing sense of apprehension that his armchair advisory shingle was morphing into an entirely new dimension. Although his personal riding skills still hovered at walk-jog with double bouncing posts any time he trotted, experience in the saddle resulted in his spousal support expanding to include what he considered important training points that in his opinion he felt she sometimes missed. Although Cindy appreciated the increasing interest he took in her riding as well as her training business, she was beginning to seriously question what her encouragement had created.

One sunny Sunday afternoon when Cindy had just finished schooling her new competition horse, it came to a head. Crimson was a bold off-the-track Thoroughbred who was almost ready to make his debut in the pre-greens. He was a flashy copper chestnut with four short white socks and elegant gaits to match his eye-catching appearance. She was crazy about the horse, taking extra time to develop his talent and sensitive temperament, sensing he had the potential to be the best she had ever owned.

One morning after filming her schooling session, Joe thoughtfully packed up the video equipment. "Not bad, honey, but you could have been a bit bolder to that last line," he critiqued, with the authority of a seasoned coach, copying the words he had heard her speak in lessons. "I think it caused you to get a bit deep to the coop."

Cindy rolled her eyes at this newest dose of his manufactured expertise, but before she could respond, one of the boarders waved from the barn. "Telephone. It's the vet returning your call about Margaret's horse."

She ran her hand along Crimson's damp neck. "After that workout, he's a bit too hot to put up yet. Joe, do you think you could hand walk him while I take the vet's call? I've been playing phone tag with him all day."

"Sure," he agreed, coming eagerly through the gate. "In fact, how about I just get on board to walk him out? You're all excited about this super horse, but I only know him from the ground. I wouldn't mind sharing your view from the top."

As she dismounted, a cautionary voice roared in the back of her head, warning her not to hand over the reins. "I don't know if that's a good idea. Trail riding old Roebuck is one thing, but Crimson is a powerful young performance horse and a very far cry from Roebuck."

Joe gently pried the reins out of her hand. "Nonsense. After all the time I've spent around you and this horse, I think I can handle a simple walk around the ring while you take a phone call. Let us men get to know each other a little better without you in the middle. Besides, after that schooling, I'm sure you worked all the yip out of him."

As though on cue, Crimson dropped his head, fixing Joe with a soft eye while he nuzzled his pocket for the sugar cube he knew he would find. "Okay," Cindy reluctantly relented. "Guess there's no harm in that. But promise to only walk. I'll be back quick as I can."

Joe led Crimson toward the three-step mounting block beside the gate before she could change her mind. "So help me get on then go answer your call."

Cindy stood at Crimson's head while Joe mounted. There wasn't a hint of grace as her husband threw his leg over the saddle, awkwardly bumping the gelding's croup with the heel of his tennis shoe. Cindy caught her breath, expecting the worst, but Crimson

73

amazingly exhibited the patience of a saint. The gelding stood quietly with polite acceptance until Joe's weight finally settled into the center of the saddle. Doubts moderately quelled by her young horse's surprisingly tolerant demeanor, she adjusted his stirrups for the sake of security, then hurried off to talk to the vet.

The window in the barn office overlooked the outdoor arena, so Cindy was able to keep an eye on Joe and Crimson's companionable progress around the rail while she talked on the phone. He held the reins casually in his left hand, stroking Crimson's neck with his right while the gelding bobbed his head in relaxation. She smiled at the serene confidence conveyed by this newfound partnership, thinking that just maybe it wasn't such a bad idea to let her husband take this baby step up another rung of the riding ladder.

But as Cindy listened to the vet prescribe a treatment protocol, her confidence began to evaporate as she kept an eye on the arena. Buoyed by Crimson's calm demeanor, it appeared that Joe had decided to take the initiative to advance their burgeoning relationship to the next level. Without warning, he leaned forward, thumping hard with both legs, applying the same awkward, heavy signal he used to ask Roebuck to trot.

Unfortunately, while Roebuck was a bombproof, tough-sided sixteen-year-old school horse, Crimson possessed the sensitivity of a high-powered Thoroughbred not long off the track. The gelding's head flew up, startled by the hard wallop from Joe's heels that was definitely not the normal soft "go" aids he was used to receiving from Cindy.

The sudden unexpected swell of power beneath the saddle caused Joe to flop backward, quickly grabbing a handful of mane for balance. Although poised for flight, when Joe stopped kicking, for some unknown reason Crimson decided to settle. The horse shook his head with what seemed to be a conciliatory shrug of acceptance, then pushed off quietly into a trot on his own accord.

Even from a distance, Cindy couldn't miss the shocked expression on Joe's face which probably mirrored hers as she watched in alarm from the office. While Roebuck had a short shuffling gait that was far from tracking up, Crimson's stride was lofty and ground-covering, something Joe had never experienced. But rather than make the smart decision to drop back into the walk before the pace accelerated, pride took over and he decided to stay the course. Cindy could only think "Amen!" to her father's wise, often declared prophecy of "Those that know not, know not what they do."

The longer Crimson circled the ring in a trot, the harder it was for Joe to find any sense of rhythm. He sawed backwards on the reins that were far too long, trying unsuccessfully to slow the horse while his own center of gravity rose higher and higher with the quickening gait. Another lap around the ring finally pushed Crimson over the edge into a ragged canter, with strides that kept lengthening the harder Joe pulled and the tighter his legs clamped on for balance.

Cindy dropped the phone in mid-phrase with the vet. She raced out of the barn, hoping to avert certain crisis. But before she was close enough to shout words of assistance, the remainder of Crimson's patience with his flailing rider unraveled. Without warning, he abruptly dropped his left shoulder as they rounded the corner. The reins flew out of Joe's hands as he flipped out of the saddle, splashing bottom-first in an ungraceful pile in the middle of a large puddle at the end of the ring. Muddy water sprayed through the air, covering him from head to toe.

Rider successfully unloaded from the saddle, Crimson immediately stopped, mission accomplished. Reins dangling over his head, he stood patiently just inches beyond the mud, unwilling to share any part of his ejected passenger's watery fate. He knowingly bobbed his chestnut head, never breaking eye contact with Joe.

By the time Cindy was ringside, Joe had propped himself up into a sitting position. Wiping away globs of mud that had cushioned his fall, he scowled back at Crimson. "What were you thinking?" he angrily lectured his unrepentant mount. "Uncivilized race horse brain! This is not the track! You're supposed to take care of your rider. What's Cindy been teaching you?"

With a sigh of relief, Cindy paused at the gate. She sensed from the scolding point of Joe's finger that the only real bruise he had sustained was to his ego. She looked across the ring at the two special men in her life. One sat mud-splattered in an inglorious heap in the middle of a puddle, ranting over the other's training shortcomings, while the other stood steadfastly by without a speck of dirt on his hooves. Crisis averted, Cindy had to smile, as in that moment she knew there was no contest as to which of them possessed the most horse sense.

CHAPTER SEVEN
PASS IT ON

G race was an English teacher by trade. Devoted to her profession for thirty-five years, she passed on her love of literature to legions of high school students. Her greatest reward was seeing the light come on in the eyes of those who caught her contagious enthusiasm for the words and stories she loved to share.

Her lifelong passion for literature was only exceeded by her passion for horses. Although she had a small barn and a three-acre pasture behind her house, the time constraints of work limited her riding during the school year to weekend warrior status. However, with the looming promise of retirement, she was looking forward to changing that part-time status to full-time devotee.

Grace's aging Arab, Jazz, was also facing retirement. So while she was invigorated by the prospect of unlimited freedom to ride and learn, Jazz had reached the winding-down stage of his life. While Grace had always hoped to achieve her riding goals with Jazz, realistically she knew she would have to continue her journey with a younger partner while Jazz could cheerlead from the pasture sidelines.

The reality of a retired teacher's pension was a definite handicap when it came to covering the price tag of a suitable new mount whose criteria even minimally met her requirements. Enter into the scenario her sister with the welcome news of a free horse to a good home in her barn. The candidate was a ten-year-old petite Arab cross with a freckled white coat named Raffy. Over the phone, he sounded like the ideal solution to her quest.

At the earliest available date, Grace drove up to her sister's barn in Cleveland to try out the horse. When she saw him standing patiently in the crossties, she couldn't imagine why anyone would be willing to let this little gem go. Cute as a button with a perky swing to his trot, Raffy had dark eyes that met her straight on. Only 4'11" herself, the fifteen-hand gelding was the perfect physical match. However, although affectionate angel on the ground, under saddle he morphed into equine eruptus. The longer he worked, the more the tension bubbled beneath his surface. While no one was launched during the test ride, the very real prospect loomed large in everyone's mind.

But despite the evident potential for adversity, Grace chose to ignore the nagging whispers of doubt from her subconscious. Raffy's cute persona, combined with the very attractive price tag of "free to a good home," convinced her that a little extra TLC combined with a change in environment would do the trick to transform him into her much-desired partner. With the utmost confidence that love and hard work could overcome any hurdle, she agreed to take him on a three-month trial, certain that at the end of the period her name would officially be transferred to his papers.

Unfortunately, once Raffy had settled into her farm, Grace quickly realized the truth to the adage that there really is no such thing as a free horse. What she had saved from her wallet was more than spent in sweat, pain, and emotional turmoil at the expense of her rapidly deteriorating self-confidence.

It didn't take Grace long to recognize and dread the recurring triggers of Raffy's launch sequence. Under saddle at the walk, all remained pleasant. Even when she initially urged him into a trot, there was no hint of trouble. In fact, the trot always began as a very lethargic shuffle around the perimeter of her riding field, unresponsive to encouraging clicks and smacks with the whip. No matter how she urged, he couldn't be kicked into a forward gear. However, fifteen minutes into every ride an unexplained switch flipped in his brain. While one moment he was plodding along in an uninspired shuffle, the very next he was violently leaping and caprioling underneath her.

Try as she might, Grace was unable to identify a specific reason or warning trigger that caused Raffy's dramatic transformations. At the beginning of their work sessions, his lazy persona never appeared to be looking for an external excuse to misbehave. However, as their ride progressed, he inexplicably morphed into a very disagreeable creature. It was as though he suffered from an internal software malfunction that caused the feisty little Arab to bubble volcanically over the edge of control. There was never any turning back until the next day's ride, when the cycle would invariably repeat itself.

More than once he had dumped her ungracefully in a painful pile along the fence line. As she lay miserably in the mud, probing her aching body for damage, he would gleefully gallop off, head and tail arched high in defiance. Raffy never quit until he had lapped the field then finally stopped, unrepentant, pawing at the pasture gate. With each misadventure, Grace found it progressively more difficult to brush off the dirt and disappointment. While she had been lucky to suffer no more than morning-after aches and bruises, her confidence was almost shattered beyond repair.

Grace was at her wits' end. She was definitely not experiencing the upward training curve she had envisioned for her post-retirement. Days in the saddle had been meant to be filled with the joy of learning and exploring new horizons with an equally eager partner. While she attempted to begin each ride on Raffy with an organized, systematic lesson plan as she had in her schoolroom days, she was dismayed to realize that her current pupil had no intention of willingly participating in the subject matter.

At the end of the appointed three-month trial, a powerful sense of self-preservation caused Grace to admit defeat and load Raffy into the trailer for the trip back to his Cleveland stable. When his owner took the lead rope with a sad sigh and an "It's not the first time" shrug, Grace realized that her misadventure had been just another disappointing turn in the revolving door that was Raffy's world.

Although Raffy's departure had saved her from further physical abuse, no words of comfort or support from friends could help Grace regain her confidence that had hit rock bottom. The training adventure that had been her long-awaited retirement goal was turning into a dwindling dream. She still did not have a suitable partner and three months of abuse by Raffy had left her uncertain that she was even up to the challenge.

A riding friend who had been the sympathetic recipient of many of her tearful nightly Raffy phone tirades offered a suggestion. Her niece, who was a professor at the local university, was about to begin a six-month sabbatical in London. She was in need of someone to care for her twenty-two-year-old Thoroughbred mare until she returned.

The friend assured Grace that Miss Daisy was an easy keeper, healthy and sound. Despite her age, she was fit and still in regular work. All that was needed was someone trustworthy to keep her legged up while her niece was away. Grace initially refused. The bout with Raffy had quashed her enthusiasm. The thought of failing with another new partner was more than she was ready to face.

However, despite the discouraging setbacks, her experience with Raffy gave her a new level of empathy for the students she had taught, especially those who struggled with her classes for a myriad of reasons. No matter their difficulties or even disinterest, she had tenaciously searched for the motivation to inspire them to reach beyond their limitations to excel.

Now she realized her own crisis of confidence due to Raffy had relegated her to the same level of paralysis as those students she always sought to elevate. If she couldn't allow her students to be defeated, how could she now allow personal failure with one ornery little Arabian to prevent her from the fulfillment of her deepest desires? Filled with renewed purpose, she called her friend and agreed to care for the mare until her owner returned.

When Grace's confidence was at its lowest ebb, she had the good fortune to have Miss Daisy step off the trailer and enter her life. The senior mare with the unusual seahorse-shaped blaze was fit and trim with a shiny coat that belied her age. The chestnut quickly settled into the farm as though she had always been a resident. She had a matter-of-fact approach to life without a hint of drama. A nose-to-nose squeal and a tail flick were all it took to become close pasture buddies with Jazz.

Whenever Grace was in the barn, she noticed Miss Daisy studying her with a deep, penetrating gaze. There wasn't a hint of mistrust or nervousness in her full brown eyes, just a warm, open curiosity that reached out across the aisle. It was impossible not to be drawn to the mare with a pat and a carrot from her pocket. Much as Grace was determined to keep her distance, she was intrigued by the demeanor of this pleasant new addition to her barn. Still, she hadn't ridden a horse since her last rock-and-roll with Raffy, so she waited a week before bringing out the saddle.

The first morning she tacked her up, Miss Daisy stood quietly, nuzzling Grace's shoulder whenever

85

she was in range. At the mounting block, the mare waited patiently while Grace nervously fidgeted with the stirrups. When Grace still remained ground bound, Miss Daisy swung her neck around, giving her a gentle, encouraging nudge on the bottom. With a sheepish smile, Grace finally stepped up into the stirrup.

As soon as she closed her legs to ask her to move forward, Miss Daisy was all business. In response to the horse's motion, Grace's nerves took over, causing her to grab the reins too short and tight. But the mare wasn't put off or agitated by the unnecessary pressure. In response to Grace's vice-like grip of the saddle, Miss Daisy patiently bobbed her neck, waiting for her rider to settle into her easy rhythm.

For the first few rounds of the field, Grace couldn't stop herself from trembling. When she was finally convinced that nothing adverse was going to happen, she let out a long, relieved breath that she realized she must have been holding ever since the first of Raffy's explosions. Reaching forward, she gratefully stroked the base of Miss Daisy's neck. In response, the mare shook her head with a playful snort, melting away the rest of Grace's uncertainty.

Smiling, she urged Miss Daisy into an easy trot that flowed rhythmically around the pasture with a soft stride that was almost too smooth to post. In a short time, they were circling and effortlessly crisscrossing the field. As Grace's confidence swelled, she couldn't resist sweeping the mare into an easy canter, something she had never dared even attempt with Raffy.

From that summer day on, Grace was excited to mount and enter Miss Daisy's classroom to absorb all the new lessons she offered. The first ride had convinced her that the mare was the consummate teacher who loved sharing her subject with a willing pupil. All Grace, the eager student, had to do was listen and allow herself to feel everything the mare had to share. The knowledge she had been so keen to attain was waiting for her on the back of this special schoolmaster who acquiesced to pass on her years of experience to yet another eager new protégé.

CHAPTER EIGHT
THE COMMUNICATOR

G rant grew up with two older brothers on a 600-acre stock ranch outside Ft. Pierce, South Dakota, dubbed the city "Where the West Begins." His father, Ed, was a third-generation Black Angus rancher who dabbled with Thoroughbreds to scratch his lifelong itch for the track. Despite the demands of the cattle side of the family business, Ed held a trainer's license for the race track. In his spare time, he lovingly worked his small string of homebred Thoroughbreds on a narrow dirt oval behind the hay barn.

Unlike his brothers, Grant didn't care much for the cattle, but he couldn't get enough of the horses. From the time he could toddle out to the barn, he attached himself to his father's side, absorbing every piece of advice that was generously offered. By the age of five, he was mimicking all his father's mannerisms right down to the drawn-out chin rub when pondering a training problem. He had even affected Ed's confident trackside swagger – although it took him two strides to every one of his father's.

Ed was thrilled that Grant had inherited his passion for horses, and even more proud of his instinctive rapport with them. Every time Grant connected with a new youngster, Ed just shook his head in amazement at the almost instantaneous bond. No matter the temperament or age of the horse, they all welcomed Grant into their personal space without hesitation. The first curious nose touch to his outstretched hand by a foal or colt in training forged an unbreakable connection that paid off in trust and an extra thrust of speed down the stretch when it mattered most.

While many of Grant's peers spent the long South Dakota winters dreaming of baseball diamonds, his anticipation was for racing. The local season was short, beginning the end of April at the Stanley County Fairgrounds in Ft. Pierce and concluding a month later at the Brown County Fairgrounds in Aberdeen. The bush tracks of South Dakota were called bull rings; their five-furlong length was shortened from traditional track distances of six furlongs to a mile. The bull rings were simple, stripped-down layouts, far different from the manicured grounds of Keeneland, Saratoga, or Hialeah Park. Instead of canopied, landscaped paddocks, the bull rings had dusty corrals where trainers legged up jockeys on backwater skittering Thoroughbreds.

During the official racing season, the narrow Stanley County Fairgrounds track was encircled by a temporary PVC pipe railing erected around the permanent rodeo arena. The smaller bull ring tracks had tight turns that intensified the action, with often as many as three laps required to make the race distance.

Afternoon meets filled the track with a breakneck pace of flying legs, flailing whips, and profane shouts as jockeys challenged for the lead. Riders rarely wore personalized farm silks, opting instead for t-shirts that matched the color of their saddle cloths so fans could identify them as they flew past the grandstand.

Riding a mount in that carnival atmosphere was not for the faint of heart; timid riders need not apply. Courage top-dressed by a big dose of luck were necessary ingredients for a jockey to survive the charge to the wire. It was a perilous profusion of speed and sport that would never make anyone rich. Purses barely topped $1,000 to be split between the top five horses. Riding fees were not a living wage, even with the addition of a winning jock's small share of the purse.

To Grant's delight, during the month of racing distraction he served as his father's appointed sidekick at the track. From the time he was a small boy, he shadowed his father, absorbing his tricks and techniques in quest of his ultimate goal. Despite the obvious dangers, Grant's greatest dream was to be promoted from sideline assistant to actually race riding in the bull ring.

At sixteen, when Grant was finally ready to make his racing debut, much to his dismay he had a growth spurt that didn't want to stop. Up until sophomore year he had been a short boy, the third-smallest in his class. That Christmas he measured a mere 5'4", but by the spring meet he had shot up to 5'6". He was still a sinewy youth with no excess body fat, but while he could control his diet, he had no power over his ever-growing frame. Although he was nearing the top edge of height for a traditional jockey, in the bull ring size didn't matter. The only thing that counted in that rough-and-tumble, speed-crazed forum was the ability to ride your mount the fastest around the oval.

To his father's delight, he broke his maiden in his second race with the thrill of a win by a neck on a homebred colt. Grant named him Comet for the one that swept over the stable the night he had assisted in his foaling. After that first victory, he chalked up a series of wins, coming through his first racing season physically unscathed in a thrilling month that ended far too soon for both him and his father.

Much as Ed hated to end their special racing partnership, he knew there wasn't a career for his son's exceptional talents in Ft. Pierce. He recognized that Grant had a gift that far exceeded the PVC rails of the bull ring as well as the family cattle business. He decided it was time for his son to follow the Thoroughbreds to the big tracks where Ed had always dreamed of going, but never could due to the responsibilities of the ranch.

A few phone calls from Ed to some old Thoroughbred connections back East found Grant an apprentice position on a farm that developed homebred stock for the track just as they did in Ft. Pierce. It was a perfect fit for Grant to settle in and build his dreamed-of career. The niche that fit him best was breaking and prepping the youngsters for the track. His new boss was amazed at his intuitive sixth-sense ability to get inside the heads of the two-year-olds. Never resorting to force or restraints, he molded even the most fractious temperaments to his will as he started them patiently on their way to a working career.

But disappointment takes many shapes. Grant's came at the end of a measuring stick. Despite the thrill of landing his dream job, his adolescent body refused to stop growing. Much to his dismay, he morphed well beyond a compact jockey-sized package to top out at a lanky 5'11".

While his height didn't affect his ability to start youngsters on the backside, it made it impossible for him to ever make the weight necessary to pilot a horse he had trained across the finish line in front of a packed grandstand. It took considerable time for him to reconcile his disappointment that he would never be able to dress in his farm's colorful orange and blue silks to fulfill his childhood dream of winning at speed on a major track.

Since he wasn't required to stay at the track to ride races in the afternoon meets, his boss gave him the freedom to develop an independent horse-breaking business. As soon as the early morning sets were finished at the track and the upcoming youngsters at the farm were put through their paces, Grant's time was his own. Over the years, he built a lucrative side business, traveling to local farms to break horses from all disciplines.

The first potential client to contact him was a middle-aged woman named Rose. She was beyond frustration over her four-year-old Quarter Horse, Samson, who gave new meaning to the word ornery. To date, she had hired three different trainers to break him, without success. All had thrown up their hands in defeat, labeling him an untrainable rogue. Each had walked away from the job with reputations a bit tarnished, but grateful their bodies had only sustained minimal damage.

94

As a last resort, Rose agreed to give Grant a try on the recommendation of a friend who was the owner of the Thoroughbred farm where he worked. Still skeptical of her decision to hire this young man with the short resumé, when the battered bronze Datsun pulled up in front of her barn, she knew she had run out of options.

Her confidence sank even further as he got out of the car looking little more than a leggy colt himself with a smooth chin that didn't seem mature enough to need a razor. She couldn't imagine how this pubescent youth could possibly have the ability to succeed with Samson where three skilled senior professionals had dismally failed.

Grant stopped in front of Rose and held out his hand with a short nod. "Thanks for giving me this opportunity, ma'am. Now if you'll just tell me where the colt is, we'll get to work."

Rose looked him over from top to bottom, taking in his short-cropped brown hair that framed a tan face lit by icy blue eyes. Despite his neat appearance, she was immediately put off by what she considered a curt young man who didn't seem remotely interested in her insights on Samson's issues. After twenty years of owning horses, she thought it was only proper that he defer to her observations, as had the other more experienced trainers on their first day. In her opinion, an exchange of ideas over a cup of coffee should be the first-day protocol to start a relationship with a new trainer.

Unfortunately, while Grant was long on horse sense, he was short on people skills. As he had known from childhood that he was far more interested in communicating with horses than their owners, developing social skills had never been a priority. If someone pointed out that his introductory demeanor bordered on rude, he would have been surprised, thinking it best to focus on the issue for which he was hired, rather than engaging in banal conversation for the sake of social etiquette.

Rose shook her head in exasperation as she led him into the barn, certain that their relationship would be a short-lived experiment. "Come this way, but just remember our phone conversation. Samson's had his way with the best horse breakers in the area. Don't take any foolish chances to impress me, young man."

The big chestnut gelding stood at his door, watching as they approached down the aisle. As Grant reached out to slide open the stall latch, Samson squealed, pinned his ears and turned his hindquarters squarely to the door, tail swishing in warning.

Rose drew in a nervous breath. "I'm not sure this is a good idea. I don't need anyone else hurt."

Grant slowly slide open the door, never taking his eyes off Samson. "No worries, ma'am," he assured in a new tone that rolled like rich honey off his lips. "You give us a little time to get acquainted. This big fellow will be just fine."

Something in that smooth tenor caused both Rose and her horse to pause, regarding him in a new way as Grant stepped into the spotlight on the stage he knew best. Rose watched in disbelief that quickly turned to awe as her usually contentious gelding slowly turned toward the young trainer with his ears pricked.

He couldn't understand Grant's words, but his deep, rolling tone gradually drew Samson forward. First one curious step, then another, until he had tentatively crossed the distance that separated them. Continuing the low sing-song voice, Grant stood his ground, allowing Samson to approach and sniff him head to toe.

Rose leaned back against the aisle wall in disbelief at the sight unfolding before her. She was afraid to speak, or even breathe too loudly, for fear of breaking this special moment of communication that she had feared might never come from her horse.

To her growing amazement, by the end of the first session Samson had allowed Grant to run his hands all over his body, never once threatening to bite or kick. Grant then picked up and stretched each of the gelding's legs, all the while trusting him to sniff his back. As a last exercise, he grabbed a handful of mane and vaulted up to lay his stomach across the gelding's back, rubbing his neck, belly and flank while continuing to croon in the same low droning tone.

Satisfied, Grant hopped down, giving Samson a final firm pat. "He'll be just fine, ma'am," he assured, stepping out of the stall as the gelding tried to follow him out the door. "Same time tomorrow?"

Rose could only nod, finding herself at a total loss of words from the scene she had just witnessed.

And that was the auspicious start of Grant's successful breaking business. Rose was quick to sing his praises throughout the local horse community. She swore that he was a genuine horse whisperer. In her opinion, there could be no other explanation for why he had succeeded so easily in turning Samson into a confident, happy riding partner where every other breaker had failed dismally.

Just as quickly, Grant's phone began to ring. "Is this the horse whisperer?" was the first question he usually heard when he answered.

While he never once claimed to be a horse whisperer, he quickly learned not to deny it, realizing it was a good business promotion. If it made the clients happy to think their horse was being trained by a character they loved from a movie, then it was okay by him as the growing myth helped pay the rent. He was certain he was no Robert Redford, but on the other hand, not one of his clients had yet proved to be Scarlett Johansson.

If pressed, he would grudgingly describe himself simply as a communicator. He didn't claim to possess any great mystical secrets learned in the Black Hills that had been passed down through the generations. He had just learned to listen to the horses. From his first meeting with a grey filly on his family's farm when he was only six years old, his father taught him they had a lot to say.

Throughout the years, he always set aside time for a Sunday evening call home. Grant's earliest source of inspiration was still the first ear he sought to hash out uncertainties or share victories. His father never failed to answer by the third ring, ever eager to hear the latest developments in his son's growing business. While it wasn't race riding on top-class tracks as they had both dreamed of on those long-ago, successful circuits of the bull ring, Grant was definitely carving a respected niche in the industry.

As he explained to his father, the problem he discovered with most other trainers was they failed to take the time to listen to the horses, or were just plain deaf to what they were saying. They spent so much time trying to impress their clients with gadgets and gimmicks that they often failed to hear the most important individual in the relationship – the horse.

To anyone who questioned how he connected so quickly with even the most temperamental horses, Grant's simple reply was, "They know I'm listening and that I believe in them."

Fifteen years into his successful training business, Grant was still driving the same bronze Datsun. It boasted an even more impressive collection of dents, as well as 187,000 well-earned miles, but it was still running, getting the job done.

"Just like me," he thought with a smile, heading inside a new client's barn, still eager to meet the next young horse who was waiting to make his acquaintance.

CHAPTER NINE
THE HORSE FAIR

T he huge Coliseum was strangely silent, as though holding its breath. Devon welcomed the stillness, savoring one of the last quiet moments of the coming days. Pausing on the second tier, she leaned her hands against the back of one of the 8,000 plush red seats that encircled the floor, knowing that tomorrow they would be filled to capacity with cheering spectators. From high-stepping Saddlebreds to rumbling six-horse hitches to sliding and spinning reiners to elegant piaffing dressage horses, the cream of the equestrian world waited in the wings to put on another memorable, entertaining event in the big arena.

Now the only sound beneath the tall domed ceiling was the rumbling churn of a big green John Deere tractor slowly circling the floor below. Only yesterday, the surface had been bare concrete still bearing the remnants of the recently-concluded home

101

and garden trade show. But overnight, all traces of displays exhibiting the latest trends in everything from aluminum siding to lawn care equipment had been whisked away to make room for the newly-installed dirt footing that the tractor now top-dressed with a fluffy layer of clean white wood shavings.

Every weekend throughout the year, the Expo Center hosted an ever-changing roster of trade shows and entertainment, displaying products and services on the Coliseum floor as well as on the wide outer concourses that encircled the building's three seating levels. As she had each April for the past fifteen years, Devon never ceased to marvel at the efficiency of the facility's total transformation from outgoing to incoming events. Even more amazing to her was that for the next three days this magnificent facility and all its features would be her domain as she produced yet another Horse Fair.

The Coliseum was the main hub that anchored the many outlying structures. Immediately adjacent stood the Arena building which also boasted a hockey-sized concrete floor that could be transformed overnight with dirt into a second riding arena with portable bleacher seating for 1,000. It was the designated Horse Fair setting for long-format demonstrations by noted trainers of varying disciplines. Beyond the arena stood the Forum building, an open-format retail booth facility with adjoining large conference rooms adaptable for lectures. Opposite the arena and forum buildings were four long horse barns. Three were set up to stable a total of 180 demonstration horses, plus their respective associations' hospitality booths. The final barn was configured as Stallion Avenue, housing a variety of breeds with adjoining promotional stalls. In addition to the decorated hospitality areas, the center of the stallion barn showcased a formal presentation ring decorated with spring flowers and wrought iron park benches where owners could stand up their elegant stallions for closer public inspection.

Devon watched a facility maintenance worker on the elevated platform midway down the Coliseum Arena just above the white hockey boardside walls. He was carefully draping bright blue bunting around an eight-foot-long table that would serve as the announcer's stand throughout the weekend. He centered a microphone in the middle of the table, then opened four red cushioned folding chairs behind it. Just as he completed the set-up, she noticed her husband coming down the aisle from the lobby to join him for a sound check.

Greg was a short man dressed in the same navy Horse Fair logo polo and khaki slacks that she wore. Despite being an avid golfer who preferred to walk the game rather than ride in a cart, his body had thickened into a middle-aged frame. He ran a hand through the graying temple of his thick brown hair, concentrating on the Coliseum worker's instructions as he handed over the P.A. equipment.

Devon appreciated her good sport husband of twenty-three years who had volunteered to man the Coliseum mic from the very first Horse Fair. Greg had been blessed with a rich radio-announcer-quality voice that never failed to keep the main arena entertainment running on time. It was a mind-boggling job to oversee thirty-two different breed demonstrations that changed every ten minutes; not to mention the six Stallion Revues that interspersed the daily schedule. Highlighting the whirlwind of constantly-changing activities was the midday Parade of Breeds, featuring one representative from every participating association circling the arena at the same time. It was potentially a recipe for certain chaos, was it not for Greg's cool head and organizational skills.

Devon sighed gratefully. Past experience with demanding exhibitors and fractious equine participants had proved that if anyone could keep the event's jam-packed Coliseum schedule on time, correctly pronounce convoluted horse names and prevent major arena traffic jams, it was Greg. Possessed of an amazingly calm demeanor and the ability to mollify the nerves of even the most frazzled breed demonstration coordinator, he ruled the mic with a steady, rich voice that had become familiar to all who annually attended the Horse Fair.

As the official voice of the Horse Fair, Greg also recorded the radio and TV promotions for the event. Together they had even written and produced a catchy guitar-accompanied commercial jingle to promote to the general public that the all-breed expo wasn't a competitive event, but rather an exciting showcase of the best in breeds and riding styles that the industry had to offer. The commercial's tag line, strummed to a catchy country beat, touted, "It's not a horse show, it's a Horse Fair and you gotta be there … you gotta be there!"

With Devon at the management helm and Greg manning the mic and media creation, they were a formidable production team. In the early years, as the Horse Fair's popularity grew, Devon had recognized the potential for her unique marketing formula to succeed in other key cities across the country. Excited by the prospect, she tried to persuade Greg to change his career path and join her dream of building a Horse Fair network. But ever-conservative by nature, he had been unwilling to sacrifice the guaranteed security of his engineering job to follow the financial uncertainty of expanding her equine marketing dreams.

"I know the Horse Fair is successful here," he argued with his ever-annoying rational logic, "but what's the guarantee that it will succeed in other markets? Maybe you just got lucky to be in the right place at the right time with this event. Who's to say it will work as well somewhere else? It's just too big a financial risk to give up my certain job security and pension which, after all, benefits you as well."

Eventually, Devon accepted it was a losing argument. Disappointed, she had long ago given up trying to persuade him, realizing she could never transform him into a risk taker. No matter how tempting the potential reward, she finally relented to being satisfied that at least he remained dedicated to donating his time to the annual production of this event.

Over the years, Greg's job had transferred them five times from Milwaukee to Sheboygan, Wisconsin, to Ft. Wayne, Indiana, to Ann Arbor, Michigan, and finally Columbus, Ohio. Throughout the disruptive nature of the moves, the Horse Fair had become the one dependable constant in Devon's life. No longer did Greg's promotions find her uprooted and the victim of relocation unemployment. With her Horse Fair, she could successfully produce and grow the event from any location in the country, only needing to travel back to Madison the weekend of the event.

With a slight shudder of pre-show anticipation paired with the usual dose of Murphy's Law uncertainty, Devon turned away from the arena prep for a final facility checklist walk-about. Her years of producing the event had conditioned her to always expect the unexpected, no matter how careful the planning. A staff member once laughed that Devon must have seen it all, from demanding vendors to inflated demonstrators' egos to disgruntled spectators. But she had been quick to hold up her hands in protest, having learned that the only real certainty was that someone or something always lurked in the wings where least expected to present a challenge to her best-laid plans.

High on her "Murphy's Law Hall of Fame" list was the Horse Fair traffic crisis in year four that had nearly shut down the Interstate in front of the facility. Mid-morning on opening day, an unexpected high number of spectator vehicles attempting to enter the facility caused a two-mile backup stretching in both directions from the Expo Center exit ramp. Her initial awareness of the problem came in the form of an angry state trooper who stormed into the show office demanding why his station had not been informed of the anticipated high traffic volume.

Unfortunately, the traffic crisis came as much of a surprise to Devon as to the state highway department. While her marketing surveys had suggested the potential for a better-than-normal attendance, in her wildest dreams she had never imagined the number would skyrocket from the previous year to actually clog the Interstate. Although a highly-stressful period ensued until the state troopers could untangle the traffic jam and funnel the cars into the Expo Center in an orderly fashion, Devon had to admit in hindsight that the unexpected overflow was a glorious problem for a promoter to experience.

Then there was year seven, when members of the local animal rights group had threatened to picket the Horse Fair over what they considered to be the unhealthy condition of a horse exhibited by the Bureau of Land Management. While the association's demonstration also included nine other adopted mustangs in glistening peak health, the protested horse was healthy, but in a rough physical condition, having only recently been rounded up from a wild herd on the range. His inclusion in the demonstration was to serve to show the audience the before-and-after effects of wild horse and burro adoption, as well as educating them as to how they could make a difference by becoming involved in the program.

Devon was aware that every year the animal rights group trolled the Horse Fair grounds, looking for an excuse to protest. In the past, they had remained quiet, lurking below the surface, but the fresh-off-the-range mustang fueled their reformers' fire with what they considered a legitimate cause to unfurl their banner. No amount of explanation from the Bureau of

Land Management representative or pacification from Devon could deter their cause. Without a solution or compromise in sight, the Bureau had generously offered to remove the horse in question from the grounds. Having nothing further to object to, the protestors slipped back into the shadows with the warning to Devon that they would remain ever-vigilant in the service of the horses participating in the event.

But the real topper for Devon's Murphy's Law hit list happened in year two. When the Expo Center staff began prepping the facility for the Horse Fair, they discovered that the giant tarp used to cover the arena footing that was stored outside had not been secured at the conclusion of the last horse event. As a consequence of heavy spring rains saturating the huge pile, when they tried to install the dirt footing in the Coliseum it had the consistency of thick mud. To Devon's horror, she arrived on site the day before the event to find the surface totally unrideable with only thirty-six hours remaining until show time.

In a last-ditch effort to salvage the event, the Expo Center rented a dozen large commercial blower fans. Set up around the perimeter of the ring, the fans ran continuously while tractors worked to turn over the mud throughout the night. Miraculously, it dried into a rideable surface a mere hour before the event was scheduled to open. Crisis gratefully averted, Devon was certain that was the day she had noticed the first grey hairs at her temples.

But so far this year, all appeared in pristine readiness; from the 400 blue-and-white-draped vendor booths in the Coliseum and Forum buildings to the 180 wooden temporary stalls set to receive the demonstration horses representing thirty-two different associations. The first retail vendors and horse exhibitors were due to begin ingress in less than two hours, after which time utter chaos would ensue. The agenda for the remainder of her day would entail assisting them to settle into place as efficiently as possible in preparation for the facility gates to open to the public at nine a.m. the following morning.

Devon checked her watch, realizing that in a mere twenty hours the first of over 40,000 boisterous weekend spectators would begin crowding through the gates. Although her advertising campaign as "the place to be for horse lovers" always created fresh consumer interest, a great percentage of the attendees were loyal repeat customers. Each year they would arrive proudly sporting previously-purchased bright blue promotional Horse Fair wear, from t-shirts to ball caps to shoulder bags.

She always delighted in running across Horse Fair apparel when not at the event. The furthest sighting from the event had occurred during a fall anniversary vacation to Acapulco, Mexico. She and Greg had taken a snorkeling side trip to an offshore island, only to discover the family sharing their boat ride to the site all wore bright blue Horse Fair t-shirts. Once they learned who Devon and Greg were, the trip was spent sharing favorite Horse Fair memories.

Her inspection rounds finally completed, Devon paused in the Coliseum's open two-storey glass lobby to watch a maintenance worker climb a tall ladder. He carefully unfurled and hung a big "15th Annual Horse Fair" welcome banner over the main entrance.

Hard to believe it's really been that long, she thought with amazement of the giant event that had grown from a tiny seed of her imagination so many years earlier.

It seemed like only yesterday that yet another of Greg's frequent job transfers on his climb up the corporate ladder had landed them in Sheboygan, Wisconsin. While he did receive the usual reward of promotion and raise, she found herself once again unemployed, uprooted and relegated to look for work from scratch in another unknown area.

The move to Sheboygan sixteen years earlier had been made even more challenging by an unexpected accident from her horse. After only eight weeks in residence, she was wheelchair bound for six weeks, followed by another six on crutches. Her recovery time was spent scouring the want ads for a new job as soon as she could walk.

As luck would have it, a local ad agency was advertising a position that was a fit for Devon. She was assigned to a team that produced a boat and resort show for a company in Chicago. While working on the event that combined recreational vendors with lectures and demonstrations by experts, Devon realized that with a few tweaks, the boat show format could easily translate to any industry. If so, she reasoned, why not the horse industry, which happened to be her lifelong passion?

And so, from an unanticipated broken leg that led to a fortuitous job in an ad agency specializing in boating and RV promotions, came the inspiration for what would become the Horse Fair, now unfurling its 15th annual welcome banner in anticipation of over 40,000 spectators who would pass beneath it throughout the weekend.

"Looks great as always, Dan," Devon called up to the man on the ladder as he attached the sign's final grommet.

"I'm bringing my kids tomorrow," he assured her. "They've been talking about it for weeks. It's their favorite event at the Expo Center. We wouldn't miss it."

"Stop by the office before you leave today and I'll give you some passes for the family," she offered. "Can't let my best fans down."

With a wave, she crossed the lobby to unlock the door to her temporary office located beside the entrance doors. Furnished with two metal desks plus an assortment of folding chairs, it would serve as control central for the duration of the Horse Fair. Although the event's never-ending demands were guaranteed to keep Devon on the run, wearing down the treads of her new tennis shoes, she knew she could count on her office manager, Josie, to skillfully handle control central in her absence.

An invaluable member of her staff from day one with fifteen years of dedicated service to the Horse Fair, Josie was responsible for coordinating the schedules of the temporary workers, as well as answering the myriad of office walk-in questions from exhibitors and spectators alike. Her greatest talent was putting people at ease as she masterfully put out the multitude of emotional and technical fires that erupted through the office door throughout the weekend.

Devon quickly unpacked the boxes of files and exhibitor packets in readiness for pickup by the first arrivals. The final items she removed were two laminated signs that always hung above her desk throughout the show in clear view of anyone entering the office. The placards had served her well, bearing sage advice garnered from years of experience. They read "Everything is ALWAYS someplace" and "There are NO Problems ... Only Opportunities!"

She had just finished taping up the final sign when Josie came through the door, precariously balancing a stack of boxes that almost hid her cheery round face. Setting the boxes on the front desk, she nodded at the signs with a grin. "Got it. No problems, only opportunities. Starting right now!"

Devon gave her longtime friend a warm hug, forever grateful for her contributions to the event's success. "Great to see you. Booths, barns, and arenas seem in good order. I think I've stocked the office with everything you'll need, but double-check me. There's still time to send someone to pick up anything I may have forgotten."

Josie chuckled. "I'm sure we're good to go. In all these years, I've never known you to forget so much as a paper clip. But as much as I'd like to catch up, you better get out to the barns. When I drove in, I noticed a few horse trailers had arrived early and were unloading in front of Barn C. Plus some retailers are beginning to line up at the loading dock to bring in merchandise to the Coliseum."

Devon took a deep breath, momentarily rolling her eyes heavenward. "And so it begins. I'm off. You can get me on the walkie-talkie if needed. Greg is down on the Coliseum floor, so he's also available once the sound check is done. However, he'll have to monitor the ring once the riders start coming in for warm-up."

Shoulders squared, Devon was out the door with a determined wave, buoyed by Josie's parting encouragement. "Remember, Devon, everything is ALWAYS someplace and there are NO problems ... Only opportunities because, after all, it's not a horse show, it's a Horse Fair ... and you gotta be there!"

CHAPTER TEN
GOTTA LOVE

T he first thing about Colin that caught Laura's attention was his contagious laugh. It rippled up from deep inside his chest, scratching the air with a mid-Atlantic rasp. Anyone lucky enough to hear it couldn't resist being drawn toward him. Always attached to the laugh was the guarantee of a rich story, certain to include a horse.

Dressed in a tailored navy suit that hung perfectly from broad shoulders, he leaned lightly against a white column at the edge of the crowded ballroom. Casually holding a glass of Maker's Mark in his left hand, his right gestured to punctuate the story he was relating to the small group of partygoers clustered around him, their laughter harmonizing under his.

Laura had reluctantly agreed to attend the party at the insistence of her friend, Gracie, who argued that a 40th birthday required a proper celebration.

Gracie maintained that the glitter of an upscale Washington party would be the perfect celebratory change of pace from the stables and dusty riding arenas where Laura had dedicated herself for more than twenty years.

While there had been a sprinkling of men throughout the years who had briefly intrigued Laura, none were able to capture her heart sufficiently to distract her from the career path she had set herself on since childhood. Her chosen sport of dressage was just beginning to gain momentum on a competitive level in the United States as she started climbing the levels in her teens. Unfortunately, experienced trainers were few and far between, with limited openings for an aspiring young protégée.

Frustrated in her search to find a trainer who could help her achieve her goals, she set off to Sweden to master her craft at Ridskolan Strömsholm, long considered a Mecca for the study of classical dressage. The Swedish National Equestrian Center had originally been established as the central military school by King Karl XV in 1868. It remained the riding school of the Swedish army until 1968. At that time the military center was liquidated, with responsibility for the riding school turned over to the Swedish Equestrian Federation who opened its doors for the first time to non-military students.

Laura was one of the first to walk through those doors, totally immersing herself in the traditions and dressage education offered by the master trainers.

After four years of intensive training, she returned to the States brimming over with knowledge, as well as a promising eight-year-old bay Swedish Warmblood gelding, ready to take her sport by storm.

The distinctive laugh bubbled across the ballroom again, cutting through the casual party chatter to recapture Laura's attention. She had to admit she found it, as well as the attractive man at its source, intriguing. His deeply-tanned face was framed by dark hair, streaked with a hint of grey at the temples. However, she was hesitant to cross the room to introduce herself to a complete stranger.

"Just who is that man with the great laugh?" she asked her friend.

Gracie followed Laura's curious gaze. "Why, that's Colin Graves. Big shot with the Thoroughbreds. Trains some of the top horses for money people. Very well connected on and off the track.

From what I've heard, he worked his way up over the years from assistant to respected trainer and breeder in his own right," she continued. "Rumor on the relationship side says years ago he had a backside fling with an ambitious exercise girl.

Supposedly it caused quite a sensation when they ran off and got married after just two months."

Laura raised her eyebrows. "Now that's a fast operator!"

"Marriage didn't last much longer," Gracie said with a chuckle. "Guess he learned his lesson, because since then, except for a few flings that made the society page, he's remained a confirmed bachelor for over thirty years."

Laura looked away with a disappointed sigh. "Too bad. That's way too much history for me. Experience has taught me to stay well clear of trackies no matter at what level they play."

Gracie was unwilling to let her off so easily. Firmly grabbing her friend's elbow, she steered her across the floor. "C'mon, let's have some fun. That's what birthdays are for. No harm in at least meeting an interesting man. That's my friend, Sue, in the red dress standing beside him. We'll get her to introduce us."

But third-party introductions were unnecessary. Colin's piercing grey eyes were distracted from his companions by Laura's approach and he never looked away. He flashed a warm smile when she and Gracie stopped beside his group. "And who is this lovely lady? I don't believe we've met."

It usually made Laura uncomfortable when unfamiliar men were forward, but for some inexplicable reason, Colin put her at ease. She had always trivialized the movie line about strangers' eyes meeting across a crowded room, but now she found she didn't want to look away.

When Laura was hesitant to respond to his questions, Gracie was quick to introduce them both. "I'm Gracie and this is my friend, Laura. We're out celebrating her birthday."

Across the room, the quartet had finished tuning up and began playing the Sinatra standard "Fly Me to the Moon." Without taking his eyes off Laura, Colin extended his hand. "No better way to celebrate a birthday. May I have the first dance?"

As Gracie watched her usually reticent friend in amazement, Laura put her hand in Colin's without hesitation, maintaining eye contact as he led her out onto the dance floor. Making a smooth turn in front of the bandstand, he slipped his arm firmly around the small of her back, drawing her toward him in time to the music.

It was a dance that was to last for the next twenty years. They were in perfect sync from those first steps, hearing the same music set to the beat of the horses' hooves that filled their lives. Neither had to sacrifice any of their personal equine passions as they settled into a thirty-acre farm built from scratch to accommodate both their businesses. While professionally, Colin and Laura maintained separation in their work, personally they doted on each other's passion, one on the track and the other in the tack.

Laura's side of the farm had an outdoor dressage arena situated next to a spacious indoor arena with twenty stalls to accommodate students plus horses in training. Colin's half was devoted to Thoroughbred broodmares, foals, and young stock being prepped for the track.

When Laura and Colin joined forces, he was in his second generation of breeding his "Gotta Shine" line. From the day he purchased his foundation mare at the Saratoga yearling sales, she never let him down. On the track, she had placed in twelve out of fourteen starts before retiring at five to a career as a broodmare. She didn't disappoint in that profession either, producing eleven offspring throughout her breeding career that included seven stakes winners, all proudly bearing the "Gotta" surname across many winning finish lines.

All the offspring were broken at the farm, then sent off to the track to begin serious training under Colin's watchful supervision. Once they made their mark, the colts were sold for a profit. But the "Gotta" girls who exhibited speed and promise returned to the farm to continue the mare line. Each year there was a fresh crop of "Gotta" foals representing new dreams nursing peacefully at their dams' sides.

Permanently retired at eighteen when a severe tear from foaling her last colt ended her breeding career, Gotta Shine now occupied a big pasture with her daughter Gotta See, granddaughter Gotta Go and great-granddaughter Gotta Dance, all heavy in foal to top stallions. There was no denying the genetic relationship, as each mare in the line bore the same jagged white star and rich bay coat that proudly defined Colin's mark as a successful Thoroughbred breeder.

Gotta Dance was the maiden in the group. She had been born at midnight on Laura and Colin's fifteenth anniversary. They had planned a romantic getaway celebration in the city, complete with champagne and dancing, when mid-afternoon the mare went into labor. Colin always tried to be on hand when his mares foaled, so formal wear remained safely hanging in the closet, replaced by jeans and work shirts to attend to the business at hand.

It was a difficult labor, lasting nearly eight hours into the dark of night and requiring the vet's resources to finally produce a healthy, strapping filly bearing the famous "Gotta" star on a finely-shaped head. Colin was ecstatic once she wobbled to her feet with a little squeal.

With a grateful laugh, he grabbed Laura and twirled her down the barn aisle, happily humming "Fly Me to the Moon." "Now that was our best dance ever to that song!" he exclaimed, dropping Laura into a low dip in front of the foaling stall then holding her close as the filly took her first tentative nurse at her dam's side.

Laura rested her head into the familiar groove of his shoulder, never tiring of watching the magical bond develop between one of his "Gotta" girls and her newborn. "Then that's what we should call her, 'Gotta Dance,' to always remind us of this very special anniversary."

Colin and Laura's lives flowed in a predictable, albeit hectic, rhythm dictated by the seasonal pulse of the horse industry. From Colin's demanding trackside ventures to Laura's busy training schedule, punctuated by clinics and judging jobs across the country, they lived a frenetic life that would challenge even the most devoted marriages. But through it all, their relationship flourished, rising above the stressful demands for their precious time.

When separated by work, they never failed to end the day with a phone call. Frequently, it had to wait until the wee hours when there was no chance of interruption from clients or horses. They would curl up in their respective beds with speaker phones propped on chests, eyes closed to savor the richness of each other's voice that quenched the thirst that grew in them during days apart. For Laura, it was always the contagious ripple of Colin's laughter that completed her day.

Theirs was a unique, full lifestyle that neither ever paused to consider might not last forever. But one morning while teaching at their home farm, Laura received a distressing phone call from the track that Colin had collapsed during a training session. No specific details about his condition were available, except that he had been rushed by ambulance to the local hospital and she should get there as quickly as possible.

Despite her immediate reaction, by the time Laura had driven the thirty miles to the hospital, Colin was gone. With a gentle arm around her shoulder, the doctor explained he had suffered a massive heart attack. Robbed of the chance to look into his grey eyes for a final good-bye or to hear that special laugh one last time, no condolence could possibly ease her overwhelming grief.

It was all so surreal and unexpected. She wracked her brain, but couldn't remember noticing any signs to indicate a heart condition. That morning he might have looked a little pale when they shared

125

coffee, but he shrugged it off as lack of sleep. He had left home with his usual wink and tweak under her chin; his gravelly laugh resonating across the stable yard with a casual comment made to his barn manager who awaited the daily instructions.

During the week that followed, Laura's friends swarmed to her side, trying to fill the impossible void with love and assistance. For once, Laura's stubborn independence gave way, allowing them to handle the daily details of the farm while she struggled to regain her footing. But finally she knew it was time to send everyone home and surround herself in the healing quiet of the farm that she and Colin had built and loved.

The evening the last car finally pulled out of the drive, she wandered down to the broodmare field, searching for a connection with Colin. She sensed his aura would always hover near his beloved "Gotta" girls. Three of the mares were heavy in foal, due the following month. They grazed in a contented little band beside the farm's granddam, Gotta Shine.

The air was still, heavy with the fragrance of the sweet bay magnolia trees blooming by the house. Laura leaned against the fence, welcoming the first hint of calm she had felt in a week. But before she could relax into the much-needed peace, she noticed Gotta Dance move restlessly away from the group.

Flagging her tail, she began to paw, then pace with growing agitation. A moment later, the mare dropped to her knees, rolling awkwardly, then scrambling up under the burden of her expansive barrel.

"Oh, no!" Laura cried, immediately going on high alert. Gotta Dance wasn't due to foal for another month, but she was well aware that the only predictability of a maiden mare was her unpredictability when the big day arrived.

Grabbing her cell phone from her pocket, she scrambled over the pasture fence, dialing the vet as she ran toward the mare. "Hang in there, girl. I'm coming!"

Ironically, for the first evening in a week, she was totally alone, having sent friends and barn workers away. The private time that she had so looked forward to now loomed ominously as she watched Gotta Dance drop to the ground again.

The vet finally answered on the fifth ring. "Laura? Everything okay?"

She tried to steady her voice. "No, Doc, I've got big trouble. Gotta Dance has gone into labor a month early. She's out here in the mare field showing quite a bit of distress. To make matter worse, I'm here alone. Can you come?'

127

There was a long pause followed by the answer she dreaded. "You know I would if I could, but I'm an hour away in the middle of a bad colic."

Gotta Dance struggled back to her feet, coat glistening with sweat in the moonlight. Eyes wide with fear of the unknown, the mare's usual gentle temperament was overwhelmed by discomfort. She nearly knocked Laura over as she spun away from her attempt to snap a lead rope to the halter.

"Don't know if I can manage this on my own, Doc. She's so agitated that I can't even get a lead on to take her up to the foaling stall."

"You'll be okay," he calmly reassured. "Wouldn't be the first foal to be born in a field. You know a maiden hasn't read the book yet, but nature has a way of working things out.

"I'll be there as soon as I get this horse squared away. Take a deep breath and remember all those foalings you've been through with Colin." And with that last piece of advice, he was gone.

The silence at the other end of the phone was broken by a deep groan from Gotta Dance as she dropped heavily back to the ground. She lay on her right side, belly and flanks convulsed by strong contractions. Laura realized to her dismay that the birth was coming so fast that there wasn't time to call anyone else for help.

She knelt at the mare's head, stroking her sweat lathered neck. "Easy, my beautiful girl," she cooed, trying to help them both find the courage to face what was ahead.

Unsettled, Gotta Dance struggled back to her feet, panting through the contractions. Almost immediately Laura noticed the amniotic sac bulging from under her tail. Quickly, she looked through the thin membrane to see a tiny hoof with its sole facing upward.

"Oh, no, no, no!" she cried, instantly recognizing the sign of a birth malpresentation. "You can't deliver your foal upside down!"

With each forceful contraction, a bit more of the foal's hoof appeared. The mare sank back to her knees, flopping onto her left side with a moan.

As Laura watched in helpless desperation, the breeze suddenly picked up, swirling the grass around them. To her amazement, it seemed to carry the calm, reassuring sound of Colin's voice. "You must get her up, Laura. Don't let her deliver this way. Get her up and make her walk to try to help the foal right itself."

Laura caught her breath, spinning around in disbelief, certain to see him standing over her, hands on hips, assuredly taking control of the crisis in his usual self-assured manner. But the only eyes staring back at her belonged to the three other mares, curiously watching the events unfold from a safe distance across the pasture.

The night air was charged with energy as the breeze continued to swirl around her. "Get her up, Laura. She can't deliver this way. Get her up and walk her out."

She heard the insistent directions as clearly as if he were reaching around her shoulders to steady her hands. Gathering courage, she sprang into action, jerking on the halter and slapping the mare's neck with the lead rope. "Up, Dance, up! We've got to get you moving, girl! Now!"

With a reluctant groan, Gotta Dance rocked to her feet, swaying awkwardly under the discomfort of her labor. The breeze swirled stronger around their legs, empowering Laura to prod the mare along. Ever so slowly, they circled the field, followed at a safe distance by the other watchful mares.

After two arduous laps, Laura noticed the breeze had stilled. She finally allowed the panting mare to stop. With trepidation, she turned back to look under her tail for a status check of the foal. To her great relief, the hoof had withdrawn back inside the mare.

"Maybe, just maybe," she prayed, too exhausted to continue fighting against Gotta Dance's insistence to drop back to the ground.

The mare groaned as she rolled over onto her left side, not to be deterred any longer from completing the delivery. Kneeling beside her, Laura held her breath as the sac bearing a tiny hoof reappeared beneath the mare's tail. This time the sole was pointing down in a proper delivery position. A moment later, the second hoof appeared, followed by a nose and a perfect head bearing a jagged white star. Within a few more minutes, the bay filly had slipped from her dam, continuing the Gotta Shine legacy and the fulfillment of Colin's vision.

As the three of them lay exhausted in the damp grass, Laura marveled at the magnitude of what they had just accomplished. Reaching toward the foal's tiny muzzle, she let herself relax for the first time since the labor had begun. At the hint of her touch, the foal's delicate lips gave her fingers a tentative suckle.

In that moment of connection, the breeze renewed, ruffling Gotta Dance's mane and swirling its cooling hand through Laura's hair. She gratefully closed her eyes, savoring its touch, knowing the only name for this special new addition to her life was Gotta Love.

CHAPTER ELEVEN
THE LITTLE MARE THAT COULD

A ndy was a university professor with two Ph.D.s behind his name and a well-endowed list of cultivated research projects that guaranteed a tenure-secured career. Nevertheless, while academics dictated the format of his days, he still clung to the private passion he had felt for horses as a youth. Incoming graduate candidates for his university research projects always had a leg up on the other applicants if they mentioned a love of horses in their interview.

Before the demands of acquiring a college education had required total immersion of both his time and finances, there had always been a pony or horse in his life. His passion was initially ignited in the rustic two-stall barn on his family's three-acre farmette where a split-rein bridle and bareback pad offered a young boy the freedom of adventures on a long-maned partner. A progression of bumps and bruises governed his early self-taught education. However, a badly broken collar bone sustained from a bolt that had deposited him into a low-hanging branch of the pasture apple tree had convinced his parents of the necessity of formal instruction.

Their concern for the preservation of his physical well-being led to lessons at the local stable. Introduced to jumping, he eagerly pursued this adventure with total obsession. Higher, wider, faster became the mantra of his teens as he and his off-the-track Thoroughbred charged around courses on the local jumper circuit.

But inevitably, college beckoned. As much as Andy excelled in the saddle, in his parents' eyes, higher education was not to be delayed or denied. Although he basked in the endless summer hours spent at the stable, he was realistic that his true profession lay beyond the show ring. With a sad heart, he acknowledged that horses must be relegated to a backburner until he was established in a career. Reluctantly, his horse was sold to help pay for college tuition, while his boots were polished and carefully stored away in his parents' attic in hope of rides that awaited him in the future.

Andy's sister, Susie, was twelve years his junior. She had always idolized her older brother, emulating most of his interests, especially a love of horses.

When Andy left home, she stepped out of his shadow and onto a horse of her own. Fandango was a petite, fifteen-hand Egyptian Arab who Susie immediately nicknamed "Fanny." The feisty little filly was bright chestnut with a classic chiseled head. She had the memorable markings of a long white blaze plus four ankle-high stockings, guaranteed to make any little girl fall permanently in love.

Although Andy's university position required him to move three states away, he cherished via long distance every step of his sister's journey with Fanny. He followed even their smallest exploits, offering advice that she was always eager to accept. An eight-by-ten framed picture on his desk of the diminutive mare mounted by his petite sister wearing an ear-to-ear grin always started off his workdays with a smile. But as Susie was destined to follow in his footsteps, the fateful day loomed when her horse passions would also have to be put on hold in the pursuit of a college degree.

As the inevitable day approached, Andy received a tearful phone call from Susie. Her voice was trembling as she sought his advice for the wording of an ad that would send her beloved Fanny off to another's hands while hers were destined to pick up books. He knew how difficult it had been for him to walk away from horses; and now here was his little sister crying out to him in heartbreak. Looking across

135

his desk to the photo of her beaming face as she sat astride Fanny, he was suddenly struck with the perfect solution.

"Put down that pen," he directed, fired up by his inspiration. "Don't give that ad another thought. I'll buy Fanny. That way, she can stay in the family."

There was a long moment of silence, then a piercing squeal so loud he had to hold the phone away from his ear with a chuckle. "No way!" she exclaimed. "Oh, my gosh! You would really do that for me? For Fanny? I couldn't dream of anything better!

"But ...," she paused. "I don't want you to buy her. I'll give her to you so I know she'll have the best possible home."

"If you insist," Andy finally agreed. "But there should at least be a contract and a minimal payment, so I'll pay you a dollar to make it official. Then when you graduate and have a job so you can afford her upkeep, you can buy her back for that same dollar. Now stop worrying about Fanny and focus on picking the right college. I'll start looking for a good boarding stable and work on a plan to ship her down here when you're ready."

Susie was crying again, but it was clear these were happy tears of his creation. "Thank you! Thank you! You're the best brother ever!"

The pleasant afterglow of eliminating his sister's heartbreak in one simple phone call carried him through the work day. It wasn't until he got home that evening and poured himself a glass of chardonnay to long-distance toast Susie's joy that he was suddenly struck by the magnitude of what he had promised. Without logically thinking it through, as was his usual protocol before making major decisions, he had agreed to the ownership of a middle-aged Arabian mare who was definitely too small for his six-foot frame. While he had always planned to one day resume riding, this diminutive chestnut was certainly not the mount upon which he had envisioned making his grand re-entry into equestrian sports.

He had ridden Fanny several times on visits home to experience what Susie shared in her letters. While the petite mare had been fun, with bottomless energy, on the flip side she was a very poor fit for his long legs, whose feet hung well below her girth line. On those rides, he had always been grateful that she was endowed with a high neck set; otherwise, at the least stumble or buck he felt certain her high croup would have popped him right off over the front end.

But raising his glass a little higher in honor of the impulsive promise made out of love for his sister, there was nothing left to do but find a suitable stable and select a career path forward that he and his new mare would both enjoy. Throughout high school, Susie had been active in 4-H, riding Fanny in a variety of disciplines from hunt seat to western pleasure to dressage. Over time, the little mare had become a Jack-of-all-trades, but master of none. Her only true aversion was jumping, for which she never exhibited any interest or aptitude – unfortunate for Andy, as jumping had always been his primary passion in the saddle. However, even if Fanny had shown a talent for jumping, Andy realized that an over-fences partnership would never have succeeded, as his feet hung so low beneath her barrel that knocking down rails with the soles of his boots would have truly been a reality.

The only discipline in which they shared a modicum of common interest was dressage. Neither had ever excelled or progressed beyond basic fundamentals, but at least it seemed a logical place to start. Decision made, Andy found a dressage training stable near campus and finalized arrangements to have Fanny trailered down to start their new life together.

From the very beginning, they made an odd pair. The partnership never failed to cause bystanders to pause and watch the mismatched turnout. Before them struggled a six-foot man with dangling legs, challenged to find his balance point atop a fifteen-hand, croup-high Arabian who traveled with her haunches perpetually offset to the right.

However, there is often no explaining the chemistry that develops between two souls. Somehow, someway, their relationship clicked. Right from the start, Andy was captivated by the little mare's strong personality. Her perky attitude reminded him of a 1950s rock-n'-roll bobby soxer in a poodle skirt.

In return, Fanny responded to his devotion with total affection and a never-say-die attitude. However, she always put her opinionated stamp on their training, never more apparent than centerline entrances at dressage competitions. In response to Andy's aids, she would come to a perfectly square halt at X, only to stomp her right hoof, then move it a foot forward the moment he doffed his hat to salute the judge. Her opinion expressed, only then would she remain stationary for as long as he required. It was her personal statement and no amount of patient schooling ever altered that behavior.

After two years of diligent training, their efforts were rewarded by qualifying to compete in the U.S. Dressage Federation's Regional Championships. Andy initially scoffed at his trainer's encouragement to attend the competition. After all, he reasoned, while he was proud of Fanny's results at the small local shows, he couldn't imagine his petite partner being competitive against the bold movement of the big Warmbloods he knew would be in attendance to compete from the Region's seven-state radius. But his trainer argued that he had justly won the right and should have the fun of experiencing the championships from an exhibitor's perspective. She persisted until he finally consented to join the group hauling to the show from his barn, if for no other reason than to cheerlead the group's effort.

With a nothing ventured, nothing gained attitude that had marked his relationship with Fanny from the start, they arrived at the show grounds prepared to do dressage battle with the twenty-eight horses in their Amateur Second Level Championship class. Not only was Fanny the only non-Warmblood in her division, but the panel was comprised of three German judges whose experience and eyes were attuned to the impressive, big gaits of their competition. Andy couldn't imagine how the judging panel would evaluate the performance of his saucy little Arab mounted by a middle-aged professor with dangling legs. He and Fanny were certainly not the silhouette of classical dressage!

As they circled the arena on the morning of the competition, a cluster of curious spectators gathered to watch the mismatched team. Andy smiled at the probing stares to which he had long grown accustomed. He gave Fanny's neck a pat, proud of the accomplishments that had carried him and his croup-high little mare to the reward of this prestigious point. He never imagined the remote possibility of this scenario the day he dried his sister's tears with the promise to care for her treasured 4-H pleasure mare.

As the head judge at C stood and blew the whistle, indicating their championship test should begin, Andy turned Fanny promptly down the center line. In response, she surged forward, seeming to sense the magnitude of the occasion. For the first time in their show ring career, she stopped in a perfectly square halt at X that didn't flinch an inch when he saluted. From there on, she puffed herself up to lay down a faultless test. From medium trots to travers to counter-canter, Fanny aptly proved she could compete against the big boys with a quality of work that could not be denied.

As the performance unfolded with harmonious precision, Fanny's gaits filled up the arena. Her dynamic energy and flawless carriage made it seem as though she had grown at least two hands as the test proceeded. The diminutive stature and unsuitable conformation seemed to vanish with each successfully performed movement.

At the end of the class, to Andy's complete joy and amazement, they stood in first place, a full percentage point above the next closest competitor. The quirky little mare with the strong opinions which she never failed to hide had risen to the occasion when it counted most, taking him to a place of pride of accomplishment that he never imagined possible.

Despite overwhelming odds, Fanny had proven that she truly was the little mare that could. As they waited in the arena at the head of the line for the awards ceremony, Andy fondly stroked her chestnut neck; his irreplaceable treasure of a lifetime for the price of only a dollar.

CHAPTER TWELVE
HAIRY BEASTS

J oan's wildest imagination had never included a horse. The closest she ever cared to come to one was painted in an antique hunting print that hung over the sideboard in her parents' dining room. With the exception of an obligatory honeymoon photo op on a flower-adorned donkey overlooking San Juan harbor, she had only ridden a horse once in her life.

That memorable event occurred the summer of her fourteenth year when she and her best friend, Kate, spent a week at Camp Warren in Eveleth, Minnesota. The 480 acres on the shore of Half Moon Lake promised forty teenage campers an unforgettable adventure of canoeing, crafts, tennis, archery, and sailing. Although horseback riding was also mentioned on the activities brochure, Joan had no interest or desire to straddle what she considered a 1,000-pound hairy beast for an uncontrolled gallop through the scenic woods.

However, when the seven other girls in her cabin voted majority rule for a Wednesday morning breakfast trail ride, Joan's thumbs down was overturned. Protest as she might, all her cabin mates thought it would be a grand adventure. There was nothing more Joan could do but grab a straw hat and sunglasses and grudgingly follow them down to the camp corral.

Based upon her lack of experience, Joan was assigned a swayback, sloe-eyed Paint named Roscoe. Wrangler Walt legged her up onto a well-worn Western saddle, then directed the toes of her tennis shoes into the wide wooden stirrups. Sensing her fear, he patted her trembling knee reassuringly. "Take a deep breath and relax, little lady. Old Roscoe will show you a fun time. He's a good ol' boy with not much run left in him. Just tag onto the end of the line and he'll follow along. He knows the drill."

Once the girls were all mounted, Wrangler Walt swung easily up on a black-and-white Pinto to lead the ride down the trail that circled Half Moon Lake. Junior Wrangler Ed brought up the rear, riding his Palomino gelding close behind Joan to make sure none of the girls had a problem or fell behind.

From the instant the ride moved off, Joan was uneasy with the sway of Roscoe's gait and his annoying habit of constantly stomping at flies. She grabbed the saddle horn with both hands for security, grateful that her mount didn't require steering. To her relief, Roscoe seemed content to shuffle along without any direction from her, his nose propped against the tail of the tall chestnut in front of him.

When the ride reached the beach that bordered the lake, Walt turned right to follow the shoreline. Without any guidance from the girls, their horses obediently followed him head-to-tail up the trail; all of them, that is, except Roscoe. The old gelding ignored the turn, stubbornly maintaining a straight line course directly across the beach toward the water. No matter how hard Joan pulled or squealed in protest for him to stop, he obstinately plodded forward.

Seeing her dilemma, Ed tried unsuccessfully to block Roscoe's progress with his horse's body. "Pull on the right rein!" he shouted to Joan. "Turn his head away from the lake. Pull as hard as you can!"

Joan dropped the left rein and yanked on the right with both hands, to no avail. In desperation, she stood in her stirrups and leaned backward, bringing all her weight to bear on the bit without results.

Finally aware of the drama unfolding at the far end of the line, Walt held up his hand for the ride to stop. Joan's cabin mates shouted encouragement over their shoulders. Their chorus of cheers gave

Joan newfound courage to pull even harder, but the old gelding continued to ignore all her attempts to turn.

"Stop him before he gets to the water!" Walt yelled to his assistant, unable to maneuver his own horse past the riders strung out behind him on the narrow trail. "That old bugger Roscoe is up to his trick again. Thought we had him cured of that water nonsense."

Junior Wrangler Ed spurred his horse forward, but it was too late to cut them off. Seeing the palomino closing in on his left, Roscoe picked up a canter, his mind made up. Within three strides he reached the shoreline and leapt into the lake without slowing down.

To Joan's horror, water sprayed over them as his hooves splashed into the lake, sloshing her tennis shoes and jeans. Still unable to steer the determined gelding, she was certain he was going to swim across the lake, drowning both of them in the process.

"Help! Help!" she screamed to Ed, who had galloped into the water right behind them, trying to bring his horse alongside Roscoe's churning legs.

But as soon as the lake water was belly level, old Roscoe stopped of his own accord. He shook himself hard from head to toe, nearly loosening Joan's death grip on the saddle horn. Tossing his head with a loud snort, he began to drop to his knees.

"Jump to me!" Ed yelled, trying to steady his horse beside the wavering Roscoe. "He's going to roll! Kick your feet out the stirrups and jump out of his way. NOW!"

Even though Joan realized the imminent danger of her situation, she was too frightened to release her grip on the saddle horn. Without a moment to spare, Ed leaned far over from his horse to grab her arm and jerk her out of the saddle at the last second. If it hadn't been for his quick reaction, she might have been trapped underneath Roscoe as he lay down to roll in the water.

A collective cheer went up from her cabin mates on the shoreline as Joan clung to Ed's arm with every fiber of strength she could muster. He turned his horse away from the thrashing Roscoe and carried her away to the safety of the beach. Even when they were out of the water, Joan was reluctant to release the security of the arm that had saved her from certain disaster.

Junior Wrangler Ed gently unclenched her fingers from his shirt as he deposited her smoothly on the beach. As everyone watched in amazement, Roscoe finally leapt up from his roll. Shaking water from his long, black mane, he galloped gleefully out of the lake. Without even a glance toward the other horses, he spun with tail held high in the air to charge back down the trail in the direction of the barn.

147

Ed jumped down from his horse to put a comforting arm around Joan's trembling shoulders. "I'm never ever, ever going to ride again!" she vowed between tearful sobs into his chest. "I don't want to ever have anything to do with those awful hairy beasts again!"

And she had remained true to her lakeside vow, never giving the species even a passing thought for the next fifteen years – until she had a daughter of her own. Now looking across the kitchen table where eight-year-old Amy was happily filling in the black outlines of horses in her *My Friend Flicka* coloring book, Joan couldn't comprehend how her only child, who was her mirror image in every other way, had come down with a raging case of horse fever.

No other member on either side of the family from siblings to cousins to aunts or uncles had ever expressed even a remote interest in the hairy beasts. So where on earth did Amy's obsession with all things equine originate? Certainly not from Joan, who had never shaken her deep- seated fear of the creatures from long-past Camp Warren days. Her husband, Joe, couldn't be blamed as the source either. His interest in sports began with a Saturday morning golf foursome and ended on the couch with Sunday baseball or football.

They lived in a comfortable suburban community comprised of homes on quarter-acre lots, where the largest animal was the German Shepherd two doors down. Growing up, Amy had no exposure to real horses. In her eight years, the only contact had been a pony ride at a friend's birthday party when she was five. There was also the ever-present Ginger, a palomino with a red braided bridle topping a cream-colored mane. The stuffed toy had rarely been out of the little girl's hand since he was unwrapped on her fourth Christmas. Every night, she still slept with his now-threadbare synthetic golden fur pressed against her cheek.

When the first unexpected hints of equine interest surfaced, Joan tried everything in her imagination to redirect her daughter toward what she considered more suitable pursuits. Gymnastics, ice skating, Brownies; all acceptable distractions that she hoped would serve as a cure for what was developing into a very severe case of horse fever. But without exception, nothing took hold. After a trial run at each of Joan's diversions, Amy's focus always returned to horses with renewed vigor.

Her every wish on evening stars, birthday candles, and Thanksgiving turkey wishbones was for riding lessons and someday a "real" live horse of her own. Even when playing games of tag and dodgeball with neighborhood friends, Joan noticed to her dismay that instead of running like the other children, Amy cantered like a horse, even switching leads with each change of direction.

The bookcase in Amy's bedroom was crammed with classic horse stories, as well as every new juvenile release that had anything to do with riding. The top shelf of the case displayed her treasured Breyer model horse collection. It had grown so large that a side table was brought in to hold the overflow of breeds and accessories.

With the passage of time, it became evident that Amy's obsession was far more than a passing childhood phase. While it wasn't what Joan ever envisioned for her only daughter, it was exactly what Amy envisioned for herself.

Reluctantly, Joan decided there was nothing else to do but find a suitable stable for lessons. She hoped that the reality of contact with an actual hairy beast, combined with the temperament and smells that Joan found so distasteful as opposed to the perfect, silky beauties that resided in Amy's bookcase, would finally get the bug out of her daughter's system. Much as Joan didn't want to ever see Amy hurt, a part of her thought that a dose of reality via a frightening experience like her own Camp Warren lake ride on old Roscoe would be a certain cure for horse fever.

But as is the case with so many well-laid plans, Joan's idea backfired from the very beginning. If Amy's love of horses had initially been ignited from the pages of her books and her plastic Breyer models, the reality of weekly contact with actual living horses that returned her affection with licks and nuzzles put her obsession over the top.

Her beginner lesson group included four kindred spirits all happily enjoying the fulfillment of their own cherished dreams. As soon as the little girls gathered in the stable, they giggled and babbled the language of horses that was totally unintelligible to their non-riding parents who were not members of their special tribe.

Joan never ceased to be amazed by Amy's courage in the saddle. While her maternal instincts frequently white-knuckled the wooden arms of the viewing chair during weekly lessons, Amy never hesitated to attempt whatever exercise the instructor requested. To Joan, she appeared so tiny and defenseless atop the broad back of a horse, but Amy was never intimidated. The size difference only made her kick harder to communicate her wishes to a stubborn mount.

Under her instructor's steady stream of approval, Amy's confidence soared. Joan had to admit she had never seen her daughter happier or more engaged.

While Amy had been a reluctant participant in the myriad of classes Joan had previously enrolled her in to try to entice her interest away from riding, on the back of a horse she became truly inspired. Watching her rapid progression from bouncing neophyte to controlled equestrian, Joan slowly began to appreciate the appeal of the hairy beasts through her daughter's eyes.

One bedtime after a lesson, Joan discovered that Amy had stuffed her dirty breeches and shirt under the pillow to keep the treasured barn scent close as she drifted off to sleep. Gently sliding the soiled riding clothes out from the bed, Joan dropped them in the laundry basket with a smile of surrender. As Amy rolled over and snuggled Ginger's furry neck against her cheek, she was certain that any dream playing in her child's head was sure to contain an adventure with the gentle bay horse that was her favorite lesson mount.

Joan was filled with love for the unique individual Amy was becoming. Now when she watched her daughter ride those big hairy beasts that had been a source of fear since her own childhood, they were slowly beginning to morph into a picture of grace and elegance under Amy's adoring guidance. Maybe it was finally time to set aside her own personal fears and the vision she had tried so hard to manufacture for her daughter. Joan had to admit the time seemed right to join Amy on what promised to be a memorable journey for them both.

CHAPTER THIRTEEN
THE MIGHTY QUIN

Q uin was a senior horse who carried his hard-earned legacy with a twinkle of pride in his eyes. Long past were his days of elegance, sporting white taped braids and a tail-coated rider around competition arenas. In his glory years, he had climbed to the top rung of Grand Prix dressage, garnering awards and the recognition of a job well done.

His official retirement ceremony was held at the region's biggest summer show as the lead-in to the evening's freestyle competition. Legions of friends and fans gathered ringside to enjoy his performance one final time. Sensing the magnitude of the event, he didn't disappoint, piaffing and passaging with his longtime rider to the appropriate *Dirty Dancing* hit song, "I've Had the Time of My Life." His final center line halt was accompanied by the celebratory pop of a cork that soaked sugar cubes in champagne for a final tasty tribute.

But show ring accolades were now a long-fading memory, paved over by the less demanding prerequisites of his latest profession as a schoolmaster. His new, equally important dance card was filled by students eager to hone their skills on his well-educated and very patient back.

For fifteen years, the mighty Quin enjoyed a rewarding partnership with his owner, Lori, climbing to the pinnacle of the competition training ladder. Hard as it was to step away from the indulged attention garnered by an elite athlete, he discovered an even more satisfying career in the teaching arena. Laying down winning competition tests took a back seat to fostering the dreams of dressage hopefuls hungry to experience the magic of the upper-level movements. All who were lucky to ride Quin would attest that a better dance partner than he was hard to find.

In all his years as a schoolmaster, he was proud to note he never lost a student from his broad back or sent anyone home in tears of discouraged frustration. Those who came to learn always experienced a thrill when they took up the contact to feel him waiting patiently at the other end of the reins. When they mounted with questions, they always dismounted with the answers percolating in their brains.

Throughout his life, in all he touched, the mighty Quin was a master of his craft. But gradually age and time took their unavoidable toll, as happens to even the hardiest of souls. In Quin's case, the culprit was Cushing's, that insidious disease of the pituitary gland. Despite a special diet and support medication, the disease began to take its toll, wasting away the once-powerful muscles that had propelled him proudly through countless competitions.

Despite decreasing physical capabilities, in his opinion full retirement was out of the question. Quin was still the consummate professional, living for his work and the adulation he received from his success. Gradually, Lori, once again revamped his lifestyle. His schedule was slowly eased back from the rigors of instructing upper-level movements to the less physical demands of basic dressage, opening up learning opportunities to a whole new level of eager students. If the downsizing of his skill sets bothered Quin, he never let anyone know, as he willingly embraced this new journey in his career with renewed enthusiasm.

Of growing concern to Lori was the effect of the Cushing's on the muscles of his hindquarters. The disease had caused an increasing weakness in his ability to rise from a roll or prone sleep. Always one to relish a good daily roll in the pasture, Quin was unwilling to relinquish this pleasure despite his growing physical difficulties.

When his debilitated muscles made it difficult to thrust upward after a pasture roll, he cleverly devised a system that shifted the muscle workload from hindquarters to his forehand. He would begin by using his extended forelegs to pull himself into a dog-like sitting position. Then, digging the toes of his front hooves into the earth, he would methodically rock back and forth until enough thrust was generated to propel himself back up on all four. The first time anyone saw this innovative standing technique, they could only shake their heads in amazement that the mighty Quin, who always made everything seem possible no matter the odds, had once again succeeded in making the impossible, possible.

However, arising in the confines of his stall after a night of sleep presented a much more difficult problem. While the pasture had the necessary wiggle room to perform his rocker lift system, the spatial limitations of the stall presented complications. If Quin rolled over in the night or lay down too close to a wall without leaving room to extend his forelegs, he had no choice but to wait for the assistance of his human team when they arrived in the barn to feed breakfast.

Many a morning they discovered him down, wedged against a wall, patiently waiting. When they looked into his stall, his big eyes would roll upward as if to say, "A little help here, please." His team would immediately spring into action. With a tug on the halter and pull of his tail, Lori and her husband, Dave, were gradually able to shift him away from the wall until sufficient space was achieved to accommodate his rocker maneuver.

But ultimately a morning dawned when he was unable to rise, despite the best motivated tugs and calls of encouragement. That fateful morning they discovered him flat out on his right side pressed against the wall, the bedding badly churned from thrashing. There was a deep gash over his left eye. The hide was sliced from his left hip as well as a cut above his hock. Lori was concerned there was more damage, but couldn't see his right side due to his position.

Eyes focused on his beloved mistress, he valiantly tried to respond to her commands as he always had throughout their long partnership. But no matter how she and Dave struggled to reposition Quin's bulky frame, he was unable to find the strength to respond.

After countless unsuccessful attempts, Lori finally collapsed in the shavings beside Quin. She cradled his head in her lap, tears running down her face onto his cheek. She looked up at Dave in defeated surrender. "He's just too exhausted. We all are. I don't think we can do it this time."

Dave gently stroked her hair. "For all our sakes, I think it's time to call the vet, Lori. We've done our best for him, and we can only do what we can do. It's time to do what's right for him now."

As desperately as she wanted to protest, she had always known in her heart that this day was inevitable. Even though all three spirits in the stall were willing, it was obvious that none of them had any physical resources remaining to succeed. There was nothing more to do but keep her beloved Quin as calm as possible until the fateful sound of the vet's truck as it arrived on the stable yard gravel.

It didn't take Doc Allen long to respond to Dave's call. When he arrived at the farm, he found them frozen in time, with Quin's big head resting peacefully in Lori's lap and Dave still stroking her hair. A quick exam of Quin's vitals and the cuts he had sustained in his struggles encouraged the vet to make one more attempt to try to get the gelding up now that he could provide fresh manpower. But despite their determined efforts, Quin proved too weak to respond. The best he could do was briefly roll up on his chest before collapsing back into the shavings.

Doc Allen thoughtfully shook his head, but he wasn't quite ready to give up on the old campaigner who had been a favorite patient for so many years. "Let's try one last thing. Although he's very weak and dehydrated from struggling and lying here so long, his vital signs are still good. I'm going to give him some I.V. fluids to see if that helps him bounce back enough to get up."

He gave Lori a long, serious look. "I don't want to get your hopes up. Quin's quite a grave case, so this is a long shot. But I want to give the fluids a chance to fortify him. I've got to make some other calls in the area. I'll check back as soon as I'm finished. If this treatment doesn't help, then we'll do what needs to be done."

As the clock ticked in Doc Allen's wake, Lori never left Quin's side and he never took his eyes off her. Through her tears, she thought she began to recognize a hint of the old strength of character that had challenged her through the years to find a way through any training struggle that confronted them. It just didn't seem to her to be the eye of a horse who had given up.

She looked up at Dave, hoping he noticed it, too. "I just sense he's not ready to leave us. There has to be a way to get him up."

Dave nodded as he surveyed the top of the stall, then looked down at Quin and Lori. "I've been thinking that maybe, just maybe, there might be something we can do. It's a pretty crazy plan, but at this point what do we have to lose?"

Lori found his guarded enthusiasm contagious, allowing a little hope to creep in. "Whatever it takes, let's try."

He handed her his cell phone. "Call Donnie. Tell him we need some construction help asap. Literally a matter of life and death. I'm going to run down the road to the lumberyard. I think they'll have everything we need. Be back soon. Keep the faith!"

Thirty minutes later, Dave and their neighbor Donnie's truck spun into the farm drive at almost the same time. Within minutes, they were carrying four fourteen-foot-long two-by-six boards down the aisle. Moving the adjoining horses into other stalls, the two men sprang into action, motivated by the urgency of the situation.

"Stay with Quin," Dave directed Lori as they set up ladders on either side of the stall. "He still looks pretty out of it, but you may need to keep him calm when we start erecting these boards over him."

Dave and Donnie worked with the efficiency of a well-oiled team that had partnered on many creative farm construction projects. They took to the job with a vengeance, knowing time was the enemy of their beloved horse who had been dangerously prone in his stall for over eight hours.

As soon as the four boards were bolted together and securely attached to the top of the header boards of the opposing stall walls, they quickly set up a come-along over the top. The tool had one hook affixed to the end and another attached to a steel cable that wound around a ratchet. The come-along was a handy tool that made it possible to lift heavy objects by working the handle back and forth.

Dave handed Lori two wide yellow nylon straps with thick metal rings on the ends. "See if you can slide these under Quin," he directed. "Position them under his chest just behind his elbows. When you pull them through, the rings should meet just behind his withers. We'll attach the hooks from the come-along through the rings. With a little luck, my system will support his weight. If it does, we just might be able to crank him up to his feet."

The three of them shared a long moment of silence, skeptically eyeing the jury-rigged contraption Dave and Donnie had constructed over a still prone Quin.

"Do you really think it's solid enough to lift him?" Lori voiced the group's unspoken doubt. "He's got to be all of 1,200 pounds. Plus he's been down so long that we don't even know if his legs will be strong enough to support himself if we actually manage to get him upright."

Donnie frowned. "Won't know till we try. I love the old bugger almost as much as you guys. I'd do just about anything to save him. But we've got to be realistic about this contraption. It could be dangerous. If the header boards break under his weight while we're in the stall trying to crank him up, there's no telling what could happen to us."

"And even if we succeed in lifting him, we don't know how Quin will react to the belly band," Dave added, voicing another serious concern. "There's going to be a lot of pressure on his chest that might cause him to panic. It's a real crap shoot, but I think we all agree it's our only chance to save him."

Despite Quin's exhausting nighttime struggles followed by the long prone period, he had remained totally coherent of his surroundings. Throughout the construction of the strange structure over his head, he remained quiet under Lori's ever-constant soothing hand; confident in the unbreakable trust that they had shared for so many years.

As though to quell any doubts his team might have, Quin rolled his eye up to meet Lori's. Instantly, she recognized the strengthening gleam of determination that had seen them through so many challenges. She gave his neck an encouraging scratch as she nodded to Dave. "He's with us. Let's do it."

She got to her feet, remaining at Quin's head to allow him a constant calming view of her. Donnie positioned himself on the opposite side of Quin's hip to help stabilize the hindquarters if they succeeded in lifting him. When they were ready, Dave squared his shoulders and started to take up the slack in the cable by ratcheting the come-along back and forth until the belly band began to tighten around Quin's girth.

At the first sign of chest pressure from the band, Quin's entire frame tensed. "Easy, buddy," Lori crooned to calm the panic in his eyes. "You've got to work with us. We can't do it without your help."

To their amazement, Quin's forehand gradually began to elevate from the shavings as Dave maintained a steady ratcheting rhythm. A few more cranks found the horse's withers up with fore legs dangling in front of the belly band. Remarkably, Quin remained calm, as though as mystified as his human team by the success of the process.

However, their joy was short lived when they realized that despite elevating Quin's forehand enough for him to get his legs under himself; he seemed unable to engage the joints and muscles that worked his hindquarters.

Despite their shouts of encouragement, he hung like dead weight from the belly band.

As they surveyed this new dilemma in frustration, unexpectedly the overhead boards gave a loud, heart-stopping crack. They gasped as one, eyes swiveling upward to see an obvious bow had formed in the middle of the four-board support structure immediately above Quin's dangling body. For an agonizing thirty seconds that seemed like an eternity, no one dared to move. But to their great relief, the boards held, continuing to support the gelding's weight without further cracks or breakage.

Without taking his eyes off the overhead boards, Dave gave a firm order to his partners. "Get out of the stall. It's just too dangerous. I'll keep the cable steady until you're safely out, then I'll crank him back down."

Lori stubbornly shook her head, unwilling to give up when a solution seemed so near. "I've got an idea. It looks like the boards are holding, so let me try just one more thing before we call it quits. Please, he deserves it for all he's done for us."

Dave looked doubtfully at Donnie's vulnerable position, dangerously crammed between Quin's right flank and the wall, but his friend nodded. "I'm game. If we give up now, he's done. What's your plan, Lori?"

She motioned Donnie forward. "See if you can inch toward his head. Try to keep him steady. Rub his neck for encouragement while I massage his hind legs. Maybe I just need to get the blood flowing from all that down time."

While Donnie and Dave breathlessly held their positions, Lori carefully began to knead the muscles along Quin's croup, working her fingers from the spine down his flanks. Gently she moved his stifles forward and back then slid her hands down his hocks, willing motion back into them with every pass of her hands.

"Oh, look!" she exclaimed when in response to her touch there was finally a hint of motion in Quin's left hock. Like Rip Van Winkle who had long been locked motionless, Quin tentatively began to test trembling muscles, trying to rediscover movement as he dangled from the come-along straps.

Lori, Dave, and Donnie's voices crescendoed into a growing wave of encouragement as Quin's hindquarters slowly began to react to her touch. Energized by their cheers, he suddenly surged forward with a load groan from deep in his gut. As they watched in hopeful amazement, the resolute gelding found his balance to stand on trembling legs under his own power, without the support of the belly band that now hung slack beneath his barrel.

Quin swung his neck around to take in his team, who were beaming at each other in exhausted joy. He shook his head, blowing hard out of his nostrils as if to clear away the pall of uncertainty that had held them all captive for so many hours.

Dave whistled softly, putting down the come-along to gently unhook the belly band. "Incredible, absolutely incredible. Whoever would have guessed that this crazy contraption born out of last-ditch desperation would actually work?"

As Quin took a long drink from his bucket, a fresh wave of uncertainty clouded Lori's newfound joy. "It's so incredible that he's up, but now we have to see if he can still walk after all he's been through."

Sensing Quin was ready, she took a deep breath and turned him toward the stall door. But any doubts she might have had were immediately erased as he put his big nose into the small of her back, playfully butting her through the door.

As Dave and Donnie watched in amazement, Lori and Quin slowly made their way down the aisle toward the indoor arena. She kept one arm draped around his neck, her other hand offering carrots to entice him forward.

Stiff and battle-bruised with scrapes from head to flank, his first steps were short and tentative. But the closer they came to the arena, a growing confidence was clearly evident to his watchful support team. Stepping through the gate, feeling the familiar sand footing beneath his hooves, he took his first full stride back onto center stage of his kingdom. Lifting his head high with a loud whinny, he served notice to let all in the barn know that he was still the mighty Quin, ready to tackle any and all new challenges – with a little help from his friends.

170

CHAPTER 14
THE SECOND FRONT

A bby hacked the big bay mare across the rolling field, enjoying the morning rays of April sun on her shoulders. When they reached the top of the rise at the back of the ten acres, she halted to relish the view that unfolded in front of her. Even though it had been two months since completion, she still couldn't believe the new grey pole barn that stretched across the front of the property was hers. Radiating from the ten-stall barn that centered the facility was an indoor arena at one end and a large outdoor sand ring at the other.

She sighed happily at the sight of her childhood dream finally come to fruition. Initially, it had been a big decision for her and Joel to uproot from the known security of home and friends, not to mention Abby's job as a department manager at Macy's.

However, the promise of finally being able to build her dream stable, enhanced by the opportunity to quit the demanding hours of her job, ultimately made the decision simple. Going forward, all her physical and creative energies could now be focused on breeding a few special mares, as well as building a small boarding business to offset the farm's expenses.

Joel's company had generously allowed them the time to get her building project off the ground while he worked out of the nearby home office. However, his orientation period was rapidly coming to an end. The next phase of his job would require long stints of international travel, leaving Abby home alone to manage the farm.

As Joel would frequently be away for weeks at a time, he insisted they hire a competent person to handle the heavy demands of the farm, from mowing to repairs. Although it was primarily a maintenance position, Abby wanted the candidate to also be comfortable handling horses in case she needed fill-in barn help. However, with Joel's first big trip scheduled in just two weeks, to date the search for the ideal candidate had hit a dead end.

Finally, the previous night Joel had come home with what promised to be an encouraging lead. "I was paying for gas at the local station when I mentioned our help dilemma to the cashier. Ironically, she said she had someone at home who would be perfect for the job. She's been trying to motivate him off the sofa for a long time with no luck. But she said he's a mechanical whiz, plus he loves horses, so she thought our job would be a great fit."

After so many unsuccessful interviews, Abby was beginning to doubt that the ideal candidate actually existed. "But what kind of experience does he have? Just because she said he loves horses doesn't mean he knows how to handle them. Any idea how old he is?"

Joel shrugged. "There was a line behind me waiting to pay, so I didn't have time to get a lot of details. My guess from the clerk's age is that her son is just out of high school. I know that sounds younger than we'd hoped, but we're running out of time and options. Let's just cross our fingers and hope this kid is the answer, even if it's only temporary until we can find someone more appropriate. I told her to have him show up for an interview tomorrow morning."

As Abby sat astride her mare overlooking the stable and pondering what project needed to be tackled next, she heard the approaching engine growl of a motorcycle. Since motorcycle traffic frequented the state route that passed her farm, she rarely paid any attention to the nuisance sound. However, to her surprise, rather than cruising by, the roar of the engine slowed as it approached, then turned slowly down the farm drive.

Just as she gathered up the reins to trot in to see what a stranger on a motorcycle could possibly want at her stable, she noticed Joel heading out from the garage to check. "He's definitely better suited than me to handle this one," she decided, turning the mare away to take a few more laps of the field.

But to her surprise, when she finished the workout and headed back in, the big black motorcycle was still parked in front of the stable. As she approached, her mare shied and snorted anxiously, sharing Abby's uneasy sentiments.

Before she could dismount, Joel walked out of the barn with a short, middle-aged man who was obviously the motorcycle rider. He wore a clean black t-shirt tucked into faded black jeans that topped heavy, scuffed leather boots. Rolled in the sleeve of his shirt imprinted with "Live the Dream Harley Builds" was a pack of cigarettes. Graying hair was neatly slicked back from his forehead, tucked behind his ears to wave at the base of his neck. He had the scraggily start of a beard that was questionable as to whether he was growing it out or had just neglected to shave for a few days.

But the most graphic images were the colorful tattoos that wove from beneath the t-shirt all the way down to his wrists on both well-muscled arms. Interwoven between exotic birds and leaf tendrils was a number eight black pool ball on his right forearm and a palm tree on the other.

Definitely feeling uncomfortable, she decided to stay mounted while Joel made the introductions. "Abby, this is Sarge. He's here about the job. I must say on our first walk-about he's got the skills we've been looking for to keep this place ship-shape. No learning curve necessary for repairs or machinery, as he's been a foreman in a machine shop. Before that he served two tours in Viet Nam as a sergeant."

His credentials were lost on Abby, who was having a hard time getting past the image of the Harley-driving, tattooed man with the cigarettes rolled up in his shirtsleeve working for them. Standing before her was certainly no couch-sitting teenage boy applying for the job, as Joel had led her to believe.

"But what about experience with horses?" she finally managed to reply, certain she had found the void in his resumé that would send him on his way. "You know that's equally as important as the equipment part of this job."

"Plenty of experience, ma'am," he answered in a twangy voice with hint of smoker's rasp. "I just love horses. My grandpa bred draft horses that he worked and showed. Spent all my summers growing up on his farm. Taught me everything he knew about them, which was more than you can imagine. Even had my own Arab trail horse before I went into the service. Sure hated giving up that pretty boy."

He sighed thoughtfully at the memory before looking back up at her. "It's been far too long without horses in my life, but I sure would appreciate the opportunity to work around them again. My grandpa always said I had a special connection with them. I'd like to think he was right."

"What work have you done recently?" Abby questioned, unconvinced that the man in front of her could possibly be the right person to fill the job.

"Unfortunately, Sarge told me the machine shop where he was a longtime foreman closed a few months ago," Joel volunteered before the tattooed man could respond. "The economy like it is, he's had a hard time finding a suitable replacement position."

Abby stared hard at her husband, incredulous that he was actually jumping to the support of this stranger who surely must be of questionable character just by the look of him. She couldn't imagine what spell the road-worn biker had cast over Joel while they had been alone in the barn reviewing the equipment.

"That's right," Sarge agreed. "The shop job dried up and my unemployment is almost out, so I need to get something new. Looks like your job would be a good fit for all of us. So glad your husband ran into my wife at the gas station."

Far from convinced, Abby dismounted and led her mare into the barn. "Well, c'mon. Let's see what the horses have to say about you."

While she untacked, she watched closely as Joel took Sarge from stall to stall, introducing him to each occupant. Much as she hated to admit it, he passed the horse test with flying colors. Even cranky old Rocky, who habitually pinned his ears at everyone, leaned his neck out over the stall door to welcome a face rub from Sarge.

"Now here's my buddy," the biker exclaimed with delight when Rocky sprayed his t-shirt with a big snort. "I can tell this guy's the king of the barn, ain't he?

"Your horses are all beauties, ma'am," he praised without taking his hand off Rocky's neck. "I'd be more than honored to groom and clean up after 'em. I can even ride a bit if you need help exercising. Never rode much English, but stick some stirrups on any saddle and I'm good to go."

Before Abby had a chance to respond, Joel spoke up. "I think we've got all the information we need, Sarge. Let us talk it over and I'll call you tomorrow with our decision."

Sarge tipped his finger to his temple. "Appreciate your time. Hope you decide in my favor. Just give me a chance and I promise I won't disappoint."

With a smile and a final nod to Abby, he strode out of the barn. A moment later, she heard the starting roar of the motorcycle as he cruised back out of the drive.

Abby finished putting up her mare without speaking until the sound of the motorcycle had faded down the roadway. "Really, Joel? Really? You're honestly serious about hiring that guy whose horse reference is the opinion of his dead grandfather? And even if he does have all those mechanical skills that he claims, I just don't think I'd feel comfortable with him as my "go to" guy when you're out of town."

"As we've learned through all these interviews, a mechanic of his caliber is hard to find," Joel argued. "Not to mention that he's got horse experience as well. You saw how your horses all naturally gravitated to him, especially old Rocky, who's not wild about anyone."

"But what about those cigarettes rolled up in his shirt?" she persisted. "I don't want anyone smoking around my barn."

"I know he's pretty rough around the edges," he agreed. "But from the time I spent alone with him, I sense underneath that coarse exterior is a good guy. Besides, I like the idea of giving a hand up to a Nam vet. Through no fault of their own, some of those guys had a really tough time of it when they came home. I have a feeling that Sarge is one of them.

"So, let's agree to compromise," Joel suggested when he sensed a hint of softening in her stand. "I'm here for another two weeks, so I say we give him a week-long trial. If after that time you're unhappy with his work or still uncomfortable, then we'll let him go. And I'll tell him up front there's to be absolutely no smoking on the property. What do you say?"

Abby frowned, but finally nodded in agreement. "Okay. One week, and be sure he knows it's only a tryout. No promises."

Two days later the trial began, with Sarge cruising in aboard his motorcycle promptly at eight o'clock. Freshly shaven and hair neatly trimmed above his shoulders, Abby and Joel found him in the barn where he had stopped to give Rocky a pat before starting work. He still wore a black Harley t-shirt, but this time there was no cigarette pack in the sleeve.

The first day, Joel stayed home from the office to establish the farm work routine. Sarge never had to be told anything twice, often suggesting a more efficient system than Joel's for some of the projects. He was even able to easily repair the broken weed-whipper that Joel had been planning to replace.

Late afternoon on the first day when his work list was completed, Sarge poked his head into the barn where Abby was cleaning stalls. "Let me give you a hand, ma'am. I've got a little more time left on the clock."

Abby looked up with surprise, not yet ready to share her space with him.

"That's okay. I've got it handled. Normally a local girl takes care of the stalls, but she called in sick this morning. Just two more to go."

Sarge put a fork in the spare muck bucket and wheeled it in front of the stall next to her. "Not a problem. You've got work that needs doing and I've got time on my hands. I'd like a nickel for every stall I cleaned as a kid, but it was always a job I enjoyed doing."

With that, they wordlessly went to work side by side, stripping out and rebedding the two big box stalls. As much as Abby hoped to find fault, when they were done she had to admit that his stall looked even better than the one she had just cleaned.

"How 'bout I help you bring in the horses from the field before I leave?" he offered when the tools were put away and the aisle swept. "Wouldn't mind spending a little time getting to know that big boy, Rocky. Maybe I could even stick around and give him a groom before I leave?"

And so the week began with Sarge arriving a little earlier and leaving a little later each day as he settled easily into the farm routine. Once the daily work list was completed, he created new projects that had Joel admiring his inventiveness. Even if there wasn't barn work on his schedule, no day ended without him spending time grooming and doting over Rocky. Although he wasn't generally talkative to people, a stream of indiscernible conversation babbled from the stall whenever he fussed over the horse. Much to Abby's surprise, the cranky old gelding who everyone considered the curmudgeon of the barn began to nicker expectantly whenever Sarge came into view.

At the end of the trial period, Abby had to agree that Sarge had proved his merit on the property as well as in the barn. "I still don't feel like I really know him, but everything he's shown us has proved you were right," she admitted to Joel. "I think it would be hard to find anyone more suitable. And he really does have an amazing way with the horses. Rocky's attitude was the final decider for me. I think the old boy's heart would break if we don't keep Sarge on. So, if for no other reason than for Rocky's sake, I agree we should make it permanent."

The next morning, Joel greeted Sarge's arrival with a handshake and a dark green shirt imprinted with the farm's logo to make it official. He quietly accepted the shirt, gently running his hand across the gold embroidered sunburst. "It'll feel real good to be back in uniform again. Appreciate your confidence. You won't regret this decision."

As the weeks and months unfolded, little pieces of Sarge were revealed by his actions, if not through his words. When he completed his assigned work, he filled the remainder of the day with projects of his own creation. He reorganized Joel's barn workshop with military precision, even setting up maintenance log books for every piece of equipment on the farm. His ultimate summer project was a sixty-foot-long garden that he tilled in beside the indoor arena. Faithfully tended and watered, he produced a bumper crop of fresh vegetables for everyone at the farm to enjoy throughout the summer.

Initially, it was hard for Abby to connect with him on a personal level. Beneath the polite, protective walls he had built around himself, she sensed a turbulent undercurrent that only seemed to still when he was around the horses. A man of few words, he never discussed any details of his life off the farm. The only glimpse into himself that he was willing to share were long-ago childhood stories of his grandfather's farm. It was through those fond memories that horses became their common bond.

One day, as Abby watched him lovingly grooming Rocky, she had an inspired idea. "When you're done today, would you like to take him out for a ride in the back field? His arthritis makes it hard for him do much more than walk anymore, but the light exercise would do wonders for his stiff joints."

Sarge's face instantly lit up with a genuine smile of pure joy that she had never before seen. "Ma'am, it would be an honor to take this fine horse out for a walk. If you hadn't noticed, me and Rocky has got a little something going."

So it was settled that each day after work, Sarge, the damaged warrior and Rocky, the curmudgeon gelding, would head down the farm lane to walk long, companionable laps around the field. Some days Abby would secretly watch their progress from the barn. While she couldn't hear their conversations, their body language spoke volumes. Her dear old gelding with the hitch in his left hind mounted by the tattooed man with the battered heart were somehow beautifully whole together, always returning to the barn with a refreshed swing in their strides.

One afternoon as Sarge was tacking up for his daily ride, Abby broached the question she had been longing to ask. "Mind if I join you? My mare could use a good long walk. It's such a beautiful day that I thought maybe you and Rocky might like some company."

At her suggestion, Sarge stopped tightening the girth, looking thoughtfully down into the stall shavings. In that awkward moment, Abby felt she had foolishly intruded uninvited into a private space where she suddenly realized she might not be welcome.

But Sarge was quick to shake off the shadow that had fallen between them. "Of course, ma'am. It is a beautiful day and it'd be me and Rocky's pleasure to share it with you."

For a several laps, they rode silently side by side around the big field, the only sounds the comforting swish of the horses' hooves sliding through the ankle-deep grass. Then with no apparent motivation, Sarge began to speak. He talked directly toward Rocky's ears, in a voice just clear enough to include Abby.

"Riding Rocky every day has been a true elixir. After more rough years than I care to remember, sitting atop this solid old boy has started to make me feel whole again for the first time in as long as I can remember."

He drew his fingers thoughtfully through the horse's long black mane. "After I finally mustered out of the service, I thought I'd left that awful war behind,

184

but ever since I came home from Nam I've felt like I've been fighting an invisible second front. No matter what I tried, I just couldn't beat it."

For the first time he turned to look directly at her, eyes full with the words he was struggling to phrase. "So many years, I couldn't seem to do anything to put things right. Nothing worked for me on any level. That is, not until I took this job on your farm. I'll never be able to thank you and Joel and especially old Rocky here for taking a chance and believing in me. I feel like this special place has given me the peace I've been searching for to finally overcome that second front."

CHAPTER FIFTEEN
FOR THE LOVE OF A HORSE

H ow great a sacrifice for the love of a horse? How much of one's self can be entwined with that soul? What limits are we willing to push to save a bond forged in love and tempered by time?

Jessie never imagined considering questions like those as she began her search for a special new horse. For years she had trained a variety of adult horses, from green-broken three-year-olds to mature campaigners. However, this time around she was in search of the ultimate experience of starting with a well-bred weanling upon whom she could put her personal training stamp every step of the process in the creation of a totally custom-made mount.

Her search for the ideal partner took countless research hours on the phone and internet, culminating in many driven miles to promising breeding farms. Those travels introduced her to a wide range of irresistible, athletic youngsters. However, while there were several tempting prospects, it wasn't until she saw the mahogany bay colt with the perfect star and white nose snip that she felt her heart strings plucked.

On that sunny summer day, standing ankle-deep in lush pasture grass, there was nothing to hint that the handsome colt wasn't the perfect culmination to her long search. From first sight, she was utterly captivated by the young Swedish Warmblood who carried the elite blood of Napoleon on his dam's side and Ricionne on his sire's. Everything before her and on paper promised exceptional potential just waiting for her training skills to unlock the champion she dreamed of creating.

When his nose affectionately snuggled her shoulder at their first meeting, she laughed that the white snip must be where the angels had kissed him before sending him down to earth especially for her. Seeing him capering at his dam's side that carefree morning, she had no idea how prophetic that statement would be.

Much to her delight, there were no red flags on his pre-purchase exam. The only slightly negative comment from the vet noted that the colt was a bit straight in both front fetlocks. However, no one felt there was any reason to worry in this otherwise exceptional three-month-old colt. Jessie was certain his was the final sign that the stars had aligned in her favor. It was time to write the check to make it official.

Prospect purchased, the next important task was to select the ideal name for the elegant bay colt that was destined to carry her dreams to fruition. As Shakespeare wrote in *Romeo and Juliet*, "What's in a name?" Jessie wanted to be sure the name she chose defined his character and influenced his destiny as well as how he would be perceived by those whose paths he crossed.

In the tradition of his breed, she wanted the name she selected to begin with an "R," representing the lineage of his sire, Richfield. In her quest for the perfect name that conveyed courage and a never-give-up attitude, she compiled long lists of places and events as well as music titles and historical figures. But, ultimately, one name kept rising to the top ... Rickenbacker.

Through research she learned that Eddie Rickenbacker was America's most decorated World War I fighter ace with more flight combat hours than any other U.S. pilot. From 1917-1919, he commanded the 94th Aero Squadron, during which time he was awarded the Medal of Honor as well as nine Distinguished Service Crosses, the French Legion of Honor, and the Croix de Guerre.

More than once his bravery stared down certain defeat, from his survival of a commercial airliner crash in 1941 to being set adrift at sea for twenty-four days in 1942 after the crash of the B-17 in which he was flying to tour the Pacific Theater of Operations in World War II. In addition to his flight exploits, Rickenbacker was an accomplished race car driver, automotive designer, and author, as well as a pioneer in commercial aviation as founder and president of Eastern Air Lines; truly a Renaissance man.

Without a doubt, Jessie knew she had found the perfectly-inspired name for her new colt as she listed the formal "Rickenbacker" on his papers with "Eddie" as his barn name, hoping he would live up to its promise. But the day she selected the name for bravery and the strength of character it represented, she had no idea how appropriate it would be for the journey upon which they were about to embark.

The next three months seemed like an eternity waiting for Eddie to be weaned and finally delivered to the stall that waited at Jessie's farm. Her gentle, retired gelding was appointed pasture mate and mentor to help the colt acclimate to his new surroundings. But in the matter-of-fact attitude that marked Eddie's temperament from the very first day, he easily settled into the farm routine as if it were his birth home.

A steady stream of friends dropped by to meet the colt who had captured Jessie's heart. Everyone was captivated by his fine physical attributes that were only trumped by his engaging personality. She would proudly turn him loose in the arena to show off his gaits to curious visitors. At the end of a romp, he would happily mug his new fan club for treats. As far as Eddie was concerned, no new acquaintance remained a stranger for long.

It wasn't until Jessie's farrier, Denny, stopped in to trim Eddie for the initial time that the first doubtful red flag arose. Instead of sharing the general consensus of the colt's outstanding type and character, he unexpectedly zeroed in on the front legs.

Denny walked around Eddie, thoughtfully rubbing the stubble on his chin. "Looks a little upright to me, Jessie. Don't want to worry you, but seems like those front hooves might want to go a little clubby. Especially that left one."

"Club foot!" Jessie gasped, momentarily reeling from his unexpected diagnosis. She had never owned or dealt with a club-footed horse. It was definitely a negative trait that had been high on her list of 'don't purchase' criteria.

"But Denny, he had a great pre-purchase exam," she protested in defense of her colt. "The vet never said anything about a club foot. The only slightly negative comment was that he was a bit straight in the fetlocks."

She paused, studying the left front hoof that still held Denny's attention. "Now that you point it out, I do have to admit he does look a bit more upright than when I bought him three months ago. But I just figured the different look was due to him needing a trim."

Denny put a knowing hand on her shoulder. "Slow down, Jessie. It may not be all that serious. Unfortunately, this condition isn't always obvious until a youngster is weaned at six to eight months of age, which is where he is now. So the vet probably called it correctly as he saw it at the time of the pre-purchase.

"Don't worry," he reassured, hoping to defuse the building concern on her face. "I've got a lot of experience dealing with club feet. We're catching it right at the start, so I think it can be managed with aggressive corrective trimming."

Jessie drew a long, thoughtful breath as Eddie gave her an affectionate bump with his nose. Denny had never steered her wrong in the ten years he had been her farrier. If he was confident he could manage this potentially damaging condition, then she would trust his expertise to make it right.

As the months passed, Jessie sensed the tendency for Eddie's left fore hoof to club seemed more pronounced. But the changes were so slight that she couldn't decide whether the condition was worsening, or if she was just overly-obsessing on it. However, with each successive trimming, Denny continued to reassure her that they were on the right track.

The second red flag of uncertainty was raised in October of the colt's yearling year. Since Jessie hoped he possessed the quality of a stallion prospect, the first necessary step was to present him at the Swedish Warmblood Association of North America's breed inspections to evaluate his potential.

The Association annually flew in two highly-qualified judges from Sweden to oversee breeding stock inspections at specified sites across the U.S. and Canada. Colts, fillies and mares were evaluated on gaits, conformation, and type to earn a place in the Association's Stud Book. The highest out of four possible rating categories was a Class I, which required earning forty-five points with none lower than a five in any single category.

Jessie trailered to the closest inspection site in Jefferson, Ohio, to present Eddie. It was his first trip off her farm in the year he had been there, so he was on high alert to all the new sights and sounds. Although it was a challenge to focus his youthful nerves and concentration, she was grateful that all her diligent groundwork had gained his trust.

The colt looked sharp for his presentation, with healthy dapples on his mahogany coat groomed to a high sheen and neat braids accentuating his graceful neck. Jessie was certain he would have made his namesake Eddie Rickenbacker proud as he stood obediently in the center of the big arena for the conformation judging. When it came time to show off his gaits at liberty, he didn't disappoint, willingly expressing his bold character and natural suspension with a special flair.

With the direction of the colt's future riding on this inspection, Jessie held her breath as the judges conferred before publically revealing their official scores. When their announcement was finally made, the silence of the arena was broken by her delighted whoop. Rickenbacker had been awarded forty-five points to earn his Class I designation, highlighted by a nine for "Type" and an eight for "Head, Neck and Body."

However, her joy was slightly dampened by the background flutter of another red flag when the head judge announced the score for "Legs." Although the colt still received a mark of seven, the comment described him as a little straight in the pasterns.

Jessie flinched as yet another expert noted this conformation shortcoming.

"Not a serious concern right now, as he is still a growing yearling," the judge explained. "But our job is to point out what we see. He is an exceptional yearling as we judge him today. However, the decision to be a stallion candidate is a serious one and cannot be made until a later date after further evaluation when he is older. If you choose to return for the next stage of inspection when he is a three-year-old, we can make a better assessment at that time."

As winter settled in at her farm, Jessie delighted in watching the purity of her growing colt's joyous escapades through the pasture snow. Leaping with the agility of a cat, then dropping down to roll snow angels, his hooves didn't stay on the ground long enough for her to notice any problems. And so for the time being, the nagging doubt over upright pasterns faded into the background.

With the coming of spring, Jessie was eager to introduce some new basic training techniques to develop her colt's foundation. He continued to prove an easy learner, eager and always willing to follow her lead. But as she began to structure his work on the lunge line, it became impossible to ignore a slight unevenness in his left fore at the trot. Despite following her farrier's advice that had progressed from trimming to corrective front shoes, it was obvious that Eddie was struggling. Jessie was beginning to learn the hard lesson that purchasing a seemingly healthy weanling didn't necessarily mean starting with a clean slate.

A lameness exam at a top veterinary clinic in Lexington confirmed that the club foot diagnosis was approaching a critical level. To her dismay, x-rays revealed rotation of the coffin bone in the left fore from the pull of the check ligament. Although the left fore had always been the primary concern, comparison x-rays of the right fore also indicated evidence of a mild rotation. The vet explained the only possibility of correction at this point was an inferior check ligament desmotomy to release the pulling pressure on the coffin bone to keep her young horse from foundering.

Fortunately, the surgical prognosis was fairly positive for a return to soundness. However, Eddie would require corrective shoeing for the rest of his life to keep the condition in check. The clinic had a podiatrist on staff who specialized in the treatment of club feet. They strongly suggested Jessie turn Eddie's hoof care over to Dr. Vern to assure the best chance of long-term soundness. Shod post-surgery with a radically set back spring-toe shoe, Jessie pledged to make the hour-and-a-half drive from her farm to Lexington every five weeks in order to give her colt every possible chance of achieving the dreams she still held for him.

Successful surgery behind, complicated but achievable shoeing system in place, and best of all, a sound horse, Jessie finally was able to proceed with her training plans. All the hours of groundwork and bonding time during surgery rehab made Eddie easy to break. By four years of age, he had embarked on a successful show ring career, to her delight earning a national ranking by the end of his first year.

Eddie's prospects proved so promising that Jessie made plans to trailer him down to Florida for some training assistance with a noted professional during the winter months. Although he had worked sound since the surgery, toward the end of the show season an unexplained stiffness had begun to develop in the left side of his neck.

Jessie decided a chiropractic tune-up was in order to put things straight before heading south. But to her dismay, in the blink of an eye from only a slight adjustment, the nuchal ligament popped out of its track behind the poll. It visibly bulged to the right side of the crest of the neck just behind his ears. Eddie flung his head in extreme discomfort, striking with his foreleg.

Gentle massage seemed to return the avulsed nuchal ligament to its proper place, but Eddie only grew more resistant under saddle as the days passed. In a short time, he became totally unrideable, twisting his neck and pinning his ears, unwilling to move forward even when free lunging.

Florida training dreams were totally out of the question. Now the only travel plan in Jessie's future was to trailer Eddie back down to the Lexington vet clinic for a reevaluation. When no obvious cause for the rarely-seen avulsed nuchal ligament could be discovered, the veterinary team suggested a nuclear bone scan to try to get to the bottom of the mystery.

Jessie was beside herself with worry at this new unexplained glitch, as it seemed despite her best care efforts that the wheels were once again coming off the bus. She realized it sometimes took a village to manage certain horses with special conditions, but in Eddie's case it was beginning to feel that he required the efforts of a major metropolitan city just to keep him together. As their years together unfolded, it became more and more evident to her that Eddie had been entrusted to her care by a higher power; one who had known she would defend him against odds that would have sorely tested even the most dedicated horse owner.

The bone scan was inconclusive regarding the neck issues, with the vet suggesting that time, anti-inflammatories and massage would eventually heal the damaged ligament. However, Jessie was discouraged to learn that the scan also revealed an unexpected recurrence of problems in the left front leg. A further lameness exam and ultrasound revealed that inferior check ligament scar tissue adhesions from the initial surgery were causing restrictions to the deep flexor tendon. She couldn't believe it was possible that they were heading back down the seemingly bottomless club foot rabbit hole, despite what had seemed to be a successful procedure two years earlier.

However, there didn't seem to be any other option but to agree to the vet's recommendation of steroid injections to the compromised check ligament, followed by a series of shock wave treatments to reduce inflammation. The vet told her if this procedure was unsuccessful, it would be possible to do a second inferior check ligament desmotomy above the original incision to release the tension and possibly clean up some of the scar tissue.

Jessie closed her eyes, dreading the thought. It seemed impossible to awake from the endless nightmare that hung over the head of her beloved horse. But despite it all, she vowed from the beginning to be in it for the long haul, no matter what it took to revive those glimpses of greatness that Eddie had shared with her in their special competition year. Like his namesake, Eddie Rickenbacker, time and again they were challenged, but had successfully stared down certain defeat. This new setback presented just one more opportunity to fight against the insidious enemy lodged in his left front leg.

The endless veterinary and podiatry costs were becoming staggering. Initially, her equine insurance policy had covered the first surgery and maintenance treatments. However, after the first year of claims, anything related to the club foot was disallowed on future policies. Now Eddie's escalating medical expenses came solely out of her personal pockets – pockets that were almost stretched to the max. But what else could she do when the beloved bay gelding with the bright, generous eyes greeted her every morning with an eager nicker for what the day ahead might hold for them? If Eddie refused to give up, how could she, when there were still options to pursue?

As his condition progressed, she built upon her top treatment team to help manage his care. In addition to the podiatry specialist, there was a massage therapist and chiropractor, as well as a holistic nutritionist who had her supplement his diet with sunflower seeds for natural vitamin E and holy basil to aid in the reduction of inflammation. She even purchased an UltraOz low-intensity portable ultrasound machine for daily scar tissue treatments.

On the day Eddie first crossed her path, she felt certain the stars had aligned to match her with the ideal horse to fulfill her long-held dreams. Time, training, and determination would surely combine to help her develop the consummate champion. But while those dreams of material victories had begun to fade with each veterinary diagnostic setback, the bond of friendship with her plucky gelding had grown far greater than any string of ribbons hanging on a tack room wall.

Now the only reward she sought for the thousands of treatment dollars spent compounded by the fears and tears and worry would be the simplicity of a pure, expressive canter around the back field without resistance. To feel the wind in her hair as they swept across the grass, leaning forward toward his pricked ears, certain she could hear the same joyful song that filled her heart in the pumping rhythm of his breath.

From the vet's serious summation, she realized they were in for another long round of therapy and possibly additional surgery. But, she was confident that by now she knew the routine and together they had become a pretty good team at overcoming the odds. Besides, with the spirit of Eddie Rickenbacker on their shoulders, anything was possible. For the love of a horse, maybe the best was still yet to come.

CHAPTER SIXTEEN
BENEATH THE BRADFORDS

F lo had an undefeatable passion for horses. In the early 1940s, she could have stepped from the pages of Harper's Bazaar magazine, comfortably clad in a brown tweed hacking jacket draped over buff-colored whipcord breeches. Nurtured from childhood on feisty family ponies, she grew through adolescent summers on neatly-braided show jumpers to autumn weekends on sturdy, first-flight fox hunters.

With a leg over the well-oiled saddle of her favorite field hunter, she immersed herself in the joy of the chase that seemed destined to stretch endlessly beyond the days of her youth. It was an idyllic existence until polio unexpectedly struck, claiming her legs in 1954. Although the doctors counted her among the lucky who lost nothing more than the dexterity of their legs, the crippling disease robbed her of her most treasured gift: to sit astride her beloved hunter.

It was a devastating blow, but as Flo fought her way back to health, she was determined not to allow the insidious disease that had crippled her legs to cripple her love for the horses that had filled her life since childhood. She struggled to shake off the unfairness of her situation, crushed that she would never again soar over fences or race across a meadow in a breathtaking gallop. But with time and the support of friends, she came to realize that for all its physical damage, the disease could never rob her of her love of horses, only the way that she would interact with them going forward.

As the long days of healing and rigorous therapy unfolded, Flo slowly adapted to the changes in her legs and gait wrought by the disease. With time and hard work, she strengthened from cautiously shuffling within the captivity of a walker to the freedom of an uneven, swaying stride supported by a brass horse-headed wooden cane. Over the years, the horse head's brass mane and facial features smoothed out beneath the ever-determined grasp of her warm palm.

What was now impossible for her astride, Flo redirected with new vigor from the ground. She became a beloved ringside fixture at local horse shows, offering sage advice to nervous juniors and encouragement to tentative amateurs. When the summer shows faded into foxhunting season, she could always be found at the forefront of the action.

Seated behind the wheel of her aging burgundy Mercedes station wagon, she carried a walkie-talkie to maintain communication with the field master as she led the string on non-riding car hilltoppers up and down country roads in pursuit of the hounds.

Fervently determined not to allow the crippling side-effects of the disease to restrict her love of the sport, she continued to maintain a personal Thoroughbred whose style suited her taste for the show ring and hunt field. All that was required to complete the equation was an aspiring junior rider who was willing to follow her tutelage. The plan provided a wonderful opportunity for an eager adolescent to pilot a quality horse in the show ring and hunt field, while in exchange Flo could live vicariously through their efforts.

The lucky girl who was chosen to ride Flo's hunter was guaranteed to grow immeasurably in experience and exposure, but she had to be willing to adhere completely to her mentor's philosophy. Flo's no-nonsense approach to training did not welcome two-way communication from the saddle. In her opinion, her training system had been successful for over forty years, so she saw no reason to open a dialog with an apprentice teenager whose primary function was to implement her instructions.

Despite, or perhaps because of, her authoritarian system, the chosen girls always thrived. Given access to quality horsepower and excellent instruction, they never failed to make an impression in competitive circles. However, once the girl aged out of the junior ranks and headed off to college, Flo was once again on the hunt for the next lucky young rider to fill her saddle.

Flo came into Kate's life when she was fifteen years old. Horse-crazed from crib to saddle, she was a constant fixture at the stable where Flo boarded her current horse, Cleanex. Kate's parents lacked the means to buy her the shiny Thoroughbred of her dreams like those that filled the picture frames that adorned her bedroom walls. However, she took advantage of every opportunity to volunteer at the local stable to earn lesson time in the saddle. Perseverance and dedication nurtured her passion into a growing talent in search of an outlet to express itself.

That dreamed of chance presented itself when Flo's current rider headed off to college, leaving her once again in search of a suitable replacement rider. On the recommendation of Kate's instructor, opportunity's door swung open through which she eagerly stepped without hesitation.

It required no coaxing for Kate to become a willing participant in Flo's master plan. Every Tuesday through Friday after school, plus Saturdays, Flo conducted her training sessions, beginning with grooming and groundwork, then culminating in the saddle. Flo always occupied her special observation station, seated on the comfort of a thick foam cushion atop a wrought iron bench in the shade of a large Bradford pear tree that stood beside the entrance to the outdoor arena. Ever coaching, correcting, encouraging; her eyes never missed a movement.

Up until she took Kate on, Flo had made it a rule to confine her relationship with the riders to the stable. However, something about this particular teenager's infectious passion and determined work ethic touched a personal chord with Flo, reminiscent of her younger self. Swayed by that special connection, she invited Kate into her life.

As time progressed, Kate's tenacity to excel through hard work earned Flo's respect. Slowly, their relationship matured beyond student and mentor as they began to generate their own personal history, founded on a true horse lover's rapport that didn't recognize age boundaries. Separated by forty-five years, they grew into an unlikely pair of best friends with horses as the great equalizer, allowing them to chatter as compatriots over the progress of a jumping gymnastic or a great hunt field run.

Most summer weekends, they chased the horse show circuit. Catching Flo's twinkling eyes as she leaned on the rail during a round, Kate knew it really didn't matter whether or not they won. Although Flo still beamed with pride whenever Cleanex was awarded a silver trophy, it was participating in the journey that gave her the greatest joy. Through Kate, she was once again soaring over every fence, regaining her feel through her rider's pure joy in her beloved bay gelding; a blue ribbon was a mere secondary bonus.

As the season changed to autumn, they chased the hounds across rolling farm fields framed by the vibrant reds and yellows of the tree lines. New to foxhunting, Kate quickly caught Flo's contagious enthusiasm for the sport, fueled by the baying of the hounds echoing through the mist of crisp autumn mornings. She rode Cleanex at the front of the field, never failing to exchange an excited wave with Flo whenever they galloped passed the car hilltoppers parked alongside the gravel roads the hunt traversed.

As their relationship flourished, the sun porch of Flo's cozy brick home became Kate's treasured sanctuary. While the afternoon sun light streamed through the bay windows that overlooked the seasonal color changes of Flo's backyard Victorian garden, they planned horse training strategy and shared dreams, both past and future. Snuggling deep into the red plaid sofa cushions, sipping ginger ale and munching on pretzels, Kate found a welcome escape from the turmoils of adolescence. Once she walked through Flo's always-open door, all problems that had seemed earth-shattering upon entering the room dissolved with good horse talk.

All too soon, Kate outgrew the junior ranks as the unavoidable time arrived to head off to college. While her parents were proud of her equestrian accomplishments, they hoped that a change of venue from the stable yard to an academic setting would redirect her life focus toward what they considered a more practical vocation. However, after four years of majoring in communications, her heart never deviated from her desire for the career with horses that she had plotted out with Flo during all those sun room afternoons.

Flo's encouragement and generosity stretched far beyond Kate's junior rider years. Whenever home on college break, Kate's first stop was Flo's sun porch, where they would reawaken their sleeping dreams of the future. Flo made certain there was always a horse available for her to ride and the opportunity to continue to develop her skills, until even Kate's parents couldn't ignore her talents in the saddle. Upon college graduation, when Flo arranged a training position at a local stable, her parents gave their blessing.

With time, Kate's passion that had swelled naturally from Flo's developed into her long-desired career, training children and developing green hunters. Aspiring junior riders now sought out Kate for the wisdom of her instruction, long ago instilled in her by Flo. As Kate's stature in her profession grew, Flo hungered for every detail which her protégée gladly supplied for the next fifteen years as her business flourished, elevating her from stable employee to ultimately owning and operating her own Willow Way Farm on twenty pastured acres.

Today, at the edge of the outdoor arena behind Kate's stable, stand two spreading Bradford pear trees that she planted ten years earlier in memory of Flo's passing. Lovingly cared for, they have grown tall and strong, casting a familiar shadow across the wrought iron bench that stands beside them. Throughout the seasons, fragrant white spring flowers to flaming red fall leaves mark the passage of time and the learning that occurs in the arena.

Most afternoons, parents sit on the bench, watching their children master the basics of the sport under Kate's patient tutelage. But in the quiet mornings, when she rides alone, schooling her horses in the fundamentals drilled into her by Flo for so many treasured years, Kate senses a warmth emanating from the bench. In those cherished moments, she can still feel Flo's eyes taking in every movement, twinkling as she reminds Kate to sit tall, look proud, and above all else, enjoy the moment ... just enjoy.

AUTHOR BIOGRAPHY

L eslie McDonald grew up in Chicago, Illinois and attended DePauw University. She is the author of **Musings of a Horse Farm Corgi, Down the Aisle, Making Magic** and **Tic-Tac**. A Grand Prix level dressage trainer with over 45 professional years in the industry, she lives on a horse farm in southern Ohio where she happily teaches lessons and writes books.

To contact Leslie, visit her website at:

http://fcfarm.com

Made in the USA
San Bernardino, CA
25 July 2016